Comments on other *Amazing Stories* from readers & reviewers

"*Tightly written volumes filled with lots of wit and humour about famous and infamous Canadians.*"
Eric Shackleton, *The Globe and Mail*

"*The heightened sense of drama and intrigue, combined with a good dose of human interest is what sets* Amazing Stories *apart.*"
Pamela Klaffke, *Calgary Herald*

"*This is popular history as it should be... For this price, buy two and give one to a friend.*"
Terry Cook, a reader from Ottawa, on **Rebel Women**

"*Glasner creates the moment of the explosion itself in graphic detail...she builds detail upon gruesome detail to create a convincingly authentic picture.*"
Peggy McKinnon, *The Sunday Herald*, on **The Halifax Explosion**

"*It was wonderful...I found I could not put it down. I was sorry when it was completed.*"
Dorothy F. from Manitoba on **Marie-Anne Lagimodière**

"*Stories are rich in description, and bristle with a clever, stylish realness.*"
Mark Weber, *Central Alberta Advisor*, on **Ghost Town Stories II**

"*A compelling read. Bertin...has selected only the most intriguing tales, which she narrates with a wealth of detail.*"
Joyce Glasner, *New Brunswick Reader*, on **Strange Events**

"*The resulting book is one readers will want to share with all the women in their lives.*"
Lynn Martel, *Rocky Mountain Outlook*, on **Women Explorers**

CHRISTMAS IN BRITISH COLUMBIA

CHRISTMAS IN BRITISH COLUMBIA

Heartwarming Legends,
Tales, and Traditions

HOLIDAY

by Rich Mole

PUBLISHED BY ALTITUDE PUBLISHING CANADA LTD.
1500 Railway Avenue, Canmore, Alberta T1W 1P6
www.altitudepublishing.com
1-800-957-6888

Extreme care has been taken to ensure that all information presented in
this book is accurate and up to date. Neither the author nor the
publisher can be held responsible for any errors.

Publisher   Stephen Hutchings
Associate Publisher   Kara Turner
Series Editor   Jill Foran
Editor   Gayle Veinotte

We acknowledge the financial support of the Government
of Canada through the Book Publishing Industry Development
Program (BPIDP) for our publishing activities.

Altitude GreenTree Program
Altitude Publishing will plant twice as many trees as were used
in the manufacturing of this product.

We acknowledge the support of the Canada Council for the Arts which
in 2003 invested $21.7 million in writing and publishing throughout Canada.

Canada Council   Conseil des Arts
for the Arts   du Canada

National Library of Canada Cataloguing in Publication Data

Mole, Rich, 1946-
Christmas in British Columbia / Rich Mole.

(Amazing stories)
Includes bibliographical references.
ISBN 1-55153-786-9

1. Christmas--British Columbia. I. Title. II. Series: Amazing stories (Canmore, Alta.)

GT4987.15.M64 2004   394.2663'09711   C2004-903750-1

An application for the trademark for Amazing Stories™
has been made and the registered trademark is pending.

Printed and bound in Canada by Friesens
2 4 6 8 9 7 5 3 1

To Jazzie, Jen, and Beth, the best "gifts" a dad could ever hope for.

Contents

Prologue

"We proceeded on up the lake, and the ice didn't appear to be too sound or too safe, so I kept testing it. I'd go ahead possibly 50 or 60 yards and I'd take the axe to get the thickness of the ice."

It was Christmas Day, 1919, in the frozen wilderness just west of what is now Burns Lake. Trappers Cliff Harrison and his brother Bill decided they'd had enough isolation. They gathered their furs, tied them up on the sleigh together with a boat, and set out on frozen White Sail Lake.

"We got up about a mile, possibly a mile and a half and the ice appeared to me to be getting very, very clear," Cliff recalled.

Then, suddenly...

"Everything just exploded. Great sheets of ice broke up in front of me and in I went!"

It was −30 degrees Celsius when Cliff Harrison's body knifed through the frigid waters of the lake. As his brother raced up with the sleigh, Cliff had the presence of mind to roll over onto a large cake of broken ice. Miraculously, the ice held his body. Within moments his brother was piling furs on top of him and began pushing the sleigh across the frozen lake toward shore.

"We've got to get to shore as quickly as we can," Cliff gasped to his brother, "because I can't live very long. Bill, I know that I'm going..."

For Cliff Harrison and his brother Bill, the desperate race against time and the elements on this terror-filled Christmas Day had only just begun.

Chapter 1
A Very Victorian Christmas

f you were to ask a handful of Canadians to think of a classic Christmas scene, it is very likely that most would describe a scene from a Victorian Christmas. Idyllic images of well-dressed Victorian families trimming their Christmas trees, caroling out in the snow, or visiting with loved ones in gaily decorated drawing rooms are often foremost on our minds when we think of Christmas. Indeed, many of our most cherished holiday traditions either emerged from or were popularized during Victorian times. Of course, not all Victorian Christmases were pleasant and idyllic. For the men, women, and children who came to British Columbia in the mid- to late-19th century, these Christmases were often filled with the hardships and challenges of trying to settle in a new land.

Furs and Farms

About 150 years ago, Victoria was merely a rude and rustic outpost of the British Empire. Indeed, if it weren't for the fickle dictates of British fashion, the fur-trading colony at the tip of Vancouver Island would not have existed at all. As it was, Fort Victoria was nothing terribly special, merely one of a number of the Hudson's Bay Company (HBC) trading posts hewn out of the wilderness.

Ironically, it wasn't the fur trade with the Native peoples who lived around Victoria Harbour that helped expand the settlement beyond the wooden stockade. It was meat and vegetables. While people in the United Kingdom wanted furs, people who lived much closer needed something much more basic — food. In the early 1850s, the HBC founded Puget's Sound Agricultural Company and established four farms within a comfortable ride from the fort. One of the closest was called Craigflower.

Kenneth McKenzie, from East Lothian, Scotland, was the manager of the Craigflower farm. In 1852, he and 20 farm hands (many with wives and children) left their homes in Scotland to start their lives anew on Vancouver Island. The group celebrated their first Christmas away from home on the open seas. They had already rounded the dreaded Cape Horn and were plying their way up the Pacific coast when December 25 found them opposite Mexico.

"Christmas kept. Grog for all hands," McKenzie noted tersely in his Royal Emigrants Almanack. Then he added thoughtfully: "Riot with Mate and Seamen." The riot was probably caused by over-imbibing, just as likely to have been brought on by boredom as by Christmas merry-making. After all, it had been almost five months since they had left British soil.

What the weary seafarers would discover the next time Christmas came around was that they would celebrate fairly riotously at their final destination as well. By all accounts, the settlers were prepared to get into the "spirit" of the season, much to the chagrin of a few.

"What are we to expect of this young, but desperate Colony of ours?" Scottish settler Robert Melrose sniffed. "Dissipation is carried on to such extremities my readers will be expecting to find nothing in my Almanack, from Christmas till past the New Year, but such a one drunk, and another drunk, and so on ... The grog-shops were drained of every sort of liquor, not a drop to be got for either love or money."

Life on the island was difficult, and the work was back-breaking as McKenzie's farm hands hacked out their homes from the forests and wrested stubborn stumps from future farm fields. Little wonder the first Christmas at Craigflower was a time for "fiddling, dancing, singing, eating and drink-ing," as Melrose reported. He added that New Year's was cel-ebrated "in a glorious Bacchanalian manner."

Glorious? Perhaps Melrose enjoyed the festivities after all. The almanac writer then borrowed a term his fellow Scots often used to describe the season's craziness, labelling it, "the daft days."

It is likely that Christmas provided a very legitimate excuse for the depletion of grog-shop stocks. Given the hardship and loneliness endured by the province's earliest settlers, drunkenness may have been inspired as much by the sweet oblivion that followed the emptying of so many bottles as by the actual celebration of the holiday season.

A Little Bit Of England

Victoria has always had the reputation of clinging tenaciously to its British heritage. That heritage and its Christmas customs were never celebrated more obviously than during the late 1800s. Holiday rituals among Victoria's "upper crust" were models of Victorian-era culture.

"Talking of Victoria today, which likes to advertise itself as 'A little big of England', I myself think it's a little far-fetched."

The speaker was Major Roger Monteith. The "today" he was referring to was 1962, when he recorded his reminiscences. The major remembered a very different kind of Victoria. Born in 1885, he grew up in an earlier era of transplanted Englishness — real Englishness. "The population of Victoria today is totally different to what it was in the early days that I remember," he continued. "In those days, you had genuine English people, born in England, brought up and educated in England — English ways, English ideas, and possibly, I might

The British Columbia Parliament Buildings, decorated
with Christmas lights, above Victoria's Inner Harbour

say, English accents." And, of course, English Christmases.

Among the many homes in late 19th century Victoria
that hosted old-fashioned English Christmases was *Pentrelew*,
which meant "The House on the Hill." Pentrelew was built
by Henry Pering Pellew Crease, one of Victoria's leading
barristers and British Columbia's first attorney general. A
mansion in the true sense of the word, Pentrelew's 33 rooms
featured expansive windows and floors covered with thick,
colourful Turkish carpets. Many were heated by large open
fireplaces. Dinner was announced by a drumstick-wielding
servant who rang an immense Chinese gong in the main

hall. There was no mistaking when dinner was served, even for those in the rooms at the far end of the enormous house. Madge Musket, Crease's granddaughter, was a small girl at the time, but Christmases in the baronial home made a lasting impression.

"We used to have the real old English Christmas dinner with a huge, enormous turkey. Being a child, of course, at the time, I remember it was about 30 pounds. We thought it was just terrific. We used to have the turkey and the roast beef and the plum pudding — a huge plum pudding — brought in by the servant, flaming most wonderfully."

Traditional rounds of visits were another of the season's cherished rituals. For Helen Hood, the daughter of BC premier and lieutenant governor E.G. Prior, English-style Christmases were usually celebrated at the 1000-acre farm of her uncle, Dr. William Tolmie. From there, they would set out to see family friends, including Roderick Findlayson, the HBC chief factor. "We'd have another lovely Christmas there and play ring-around-the-rosie and kiss-in-the-ring and blindman's buff and musical chairs. They were real old-fashion Christmases, you know, there were huge, big turkeys and huge plum puddings and umpteen things to drink — the table loaded down!"

At the home of Dr. John Sebastian Helmcken, the colony's first physician, Christmas dinner was always a family affair. Among those at the table was the doctor's granddaughter, later Mrs. Cecilia Bullen. "It was a family dinner always,

A Very Victorian Christmas

New Year's dinner at the Helmcken House in Victoria.
Dr. J. S. Helmcken is seated at the head of the table.

you see — always 20 or more sat down to this enormous
great table," she later recalled. "The dinner was simply — I
don't know — I think you'd call it, *prodigious*. How we ever
got through it I don't know, but we always started off with
oyster patties." Soup followed, and then an enormous roast
turkey and a goose. Rounding out the sumptuous dinner
were chicken, ham, mountains of vegetables, plum pudding,
enormous mince tarts, and fruit of all sorts — mostly dried.

After the dinner and its obligatory toasts, the entire
family sang around the piano in the Helmcken drawing
room. Then they were called back into the dining room
where a colossal Christmas tree stood. The tree was pushed

into another room so everyone could dance. "I tell you, it was quite a night," Cecelia said. "How the mothers survived, I don't know."

The door of the doctor's old wooden house — still preserved, on the grounds of the Royal British Columbia Museum — was thrown open to the public at large every New Year's. This tradition began soon after the doctor arrived at the fort, in 1850, and it lasted for decades.

"Grandfather held open house and anyone who wanted to come was very welcome," Cecilia remembered. "The dining room had an enormous long table. You never would have what people nowadays call a buffet supper. Everyone had to be seated every time, and we very often had to set the table about four or five times for all the people. Then, when it actually came to midnight, we were all expected to gather in the dining room — and really, there was never enough room, some had to be outside — and then we all had to sing Auld Lang Syne."

An HMS Christmas

Then, as now, Victoria was a navy town. In this bygone era, however, it was the Royal Navy. Christmas was a particularly important time for the ratings and officers "serving of her majesty" in one of the empire's far-flung ports. The men who served were on the West Coast for so long — four years — that they were allowed to bring their families out from England. Accommodation was provided for them in Esquimalt's rows of naval housing.

The navy was a great asset to the city financially. The supply of necessary provisions for the seamen generated income for local merchants. And the sailors, naturally, spent their pay at various local establishments.

"My Dad, he catered to the ships, supplied them with hardtack," remembered Hamilton Smith, whose father owned both a bakery and a hardtack factory. "He took me down in a two-wheeled cart. The road to Esquimalt was only a trail in those days and it was pretty tough going for a horse and cart."

Christmas was a busy time for the Smiths, with ships such as HMS *Royal Arthur* and HMS *Imperieuse* stationed on the West Coast. At Christmastime, every sailor would receive a fruitcake, courtesy of the Royal Navy. Sometimes the Smiths had to supply five ships — a lot of fruitcake for one Christmas.

During Yuletide, the Royal Navy made more than an economic contribution to the city, it made a cultural and entertainment splash, as well. "Oh yes," Madge Muskett recalled. "They used to put on the most wonderful shows in what was called the 'sail loft' out in Esquimalt. The sailors would put on one show one night — oh, frightfully amusing — and then the officers would also put one on another time ... songs, dances and plays ..."

At this time, these were the real thing — genuine English people. With as much style and energy as possible, in what

Officers of the HMS *Warspite* in their 1901 Christmas pantomime
"Robinson Crusoe" or "The Tale of the Treasure"

those back home in Britain would have called an outpost of
the empire upon which the sun never set, they created for
themselves a very English Christmas.

Having a Merry Mikan Christmas

One of the Christmas traditions that many baby boomers
recall with affection from their early childhoods in the 1950s
was the moment Dad pried open the two slats on the top of
the small wooden box of Japanese oranges. Wrapped individ-

ually in thin green paper, these oranges were a once-a-year treat. Now, over half a century later, in thousands of basement workshops or on crowded garage shelves, the small wooden boxes — now dulled with age and full of small tools, balls of twine, nails, and odds and ends — are subtle reminders of those post-war Christmas mornings of wettums dolls, meccano sets, Rupert books, and Lionel electric trains. Today, while the oranges arrive in recyclable cardboard containers, they are still viewed by many as a decidedly Christmas treat.

In Japan, mandarin oranges are called *mikan*, and the first ones made their way to British Columbia in 1884, thanks to a clever Japanese merchant in Victoria who sent for a Christmastime supply. Perhaps it wasn't really cleverness. Like the rituals and keepsakes treasured by other immigrants, perhaps the *mikan* was just a bit of seasonal remembrance of a former home across the Pacific. However, the delicious fruit soon found its way beyond the city's "old town" — and beyond Victoria. Nowhere else outside of Asia is the Japanese orange enjoyed more than here, in British Columbia.

Yuletide Courtship
In the late 1800s, a happy group of BC residents was celebrating the newly laid tracks of the Shuswap & Okanagan Railway. Compared to the mammoth Canadian Pacific Railway, the Shuswap & Okanagan Railway was a tiny operation, but no less important to the people in the north end of the Okanagan Valley, where stagecoaches still bounced

over the dusty, rutted roads until winter snows made them impassable, and stern-wheelers churned the lake between Vernon and Penticton. The new railway, along with the stagecoaches and stern-wheelers, helped to banish the isolation of the Okanagan Valley, but travel was still a tedious endurance test.

Alice Barrett passed that endurance test in the spring of 1891, when, after an uncomfortable five-day train trip from Ontario, she stepped onto the station platform in Sicamous, BC, and into the arms of her brother, Harry. A confirmed spinster at the age of 29, Alice had left the comfortable home of her large and affluent family at Harry's urgings. He and their Uncle Henry were working hard to establish the 320-acre Mountain Meadow Ranch, north of Otter Lake in the Spallumcheen. Taking care of the ranch left the two bachelors with little time, energy, or inclination to care for the house. Much to Alice's surprise, "the house," turned out to be a very simple three-room cabin. For the better part of the next two years, Alice would "rough it."

Four days before her first Christmas at Mountain Meadow, Alice's uncle was "up at the shop all day ... making a sleigh," while she was busy making plans and extending invitations for a Christmas party. However, arduous winter travel made those plans tenuous, at best.

"My Xmas party is rather uncertain, no-one but the Hardings and Mr. Parke having accepted positively," Alice wrote in her journal. "It is a little provoking — I'd like to know, but it can't be helped. It has been snowing all day today — the roads are good now — but no mail has come up again tonight — the track is too heavy from Sicamous for the hand-car to run. I suppose they will send an engine ..."

Mr. Parke's acceptance for a stay-over at Christmas was no surprise — at least, not to Harry. Freight-handler Harold Randolph Parke had first met Alice a month after she arrived and had cunningly arranged with her brother to make the ranch an overnight wagon stop. His long, slow courtship of Miss Barrett had begun. Alice confessed to her journal that she "did not care for his appearance — a short, fair man, partly bald and evidently over forty." He was 45, actually, but, as Alice was soon to discover, Hal's age and physical appearance concealed an adventurous spirit.

A student of Upper Canada College in the 1860s, Hal Parke had run away to join the Confederate forces in the American Civil War. During the war, he was wounded and later brought back home by his infuriated father. But a university degree and a comfortable position at his older brother's London, Ontario, law firm weren't going to quench Hal's thirst for adventure. The West beckoned. Hal packed up again and became the 100th member of the newly formed North-West Mounted Police. Sometime later, he witnessed an historic meeting with Sitting Bull. Now, he was one of the many enthusiastic, hard-working optimists who were making a future for themselves in the rapidly developing Okanagan Valley.

As Alice prepared her first Christmas dinner in the Okanagan, her brother, Harry, was more of a help than she expected. "Dear old Harry! He has been so good to me today, baked a splendid lot of bread today — twelve loaves! — and picked the chickens, for our turkey has proved a vain illusion — fancy a Christmas without a turkey.

"We are going to try and have a jolly one, though."

And jolly it was! Just in time, at midnight on Christmas Eve, Harry arrived back with "letters and parcels from home." The stage had got through! The household awoke early on Christmas Day, and they all opened their presents to and from each other — Harold Parke presenting Alice with a pair of embroidered, buckskin gloves — and from those far away in Dover, Ontario. Dinner was splendid for the seven who eventually sat down at the table that afternoon. Afterwards, Alice would recall, "We had quite a gay time in the evening playing games and acting as if we were young and jolly. Uncle actually joined in, though he pretended he would rather read."

Hal missed no opportunities. On Boxing Day, Alice wrote, "Harold and I took a little drive to Armstrong. It was a beautiful morning — sleighing perfect — the trees bending over with snow wreaths hanging from every twig, even the ugly barbed wire fences beautified by their festoons of snow."

When Alice returned to Ontario to be with her family, Harold followed. Finally, after many refusals, Alice said yes to Harold Parke's persistent proposals and in 1893, the couple was married. Not long afterward, they returned to the Okanagan Valley.

The Christmas Mail

Eventually, Harold Parke would become Vernon's postmaster, managing the important business of the town's narrow, two-storey brick post office on Barnard Avenue. In the days before automobiles, paved roads, and telephones, the postal service assumed an importance that is difficult to comprehend in our cell-phone-and-email era. Mail was the crucial link — usually the only link — between people who may have lived only a few kilometres from one another, but who sometimes travelled entire days to visit together. Given mail's vital importance, it is not surprising that Postmaster Parke and his wife, Alice, became well-known and respected figures in Vernon's business and social circles.

Again and again, in diaries (including those of Alice Barrett), letters, and reminiscences, the desperate hope for and exciting receipt of parcels and letters were recurring themes, and never more so than at Christmas, when nobody was sure when — or even if — the cherished mail would get through.

In December 1883, the few hundred residents of Kamloops were particularly despondent. "The mail has gone astray," reported the *Inland Sentinel*, "our letters have not arrived, they have most likely gone somewhere else,

e are bringing Christmas
cheer to you

A traditional Christmas greeting from British Columbia's past

up-country, perhaps, to wish a Merry Christmas to the people of Barkerville."

Up the Stikine River, about 225 kilometres from the coast, a handful of people braved the winter in tiny Telegraph Creek. The tenuous tie with friends and loved ones was a twice-monthly mail trip by sled from Carcross, Yukon. Once the telegraph lines were strung up, everyone followed the dog-team's progress as telegraphers relayed the arrival and departure from the stations the team passed along its way.

A Mingling of Traditions

Alice was puzzled, to say the least. It was Christmas, 1894.

By then, Alice was no longer "Miss Barrett," but "Mrs. Parke," married to a man on the rise — the city's assessment officer and then assistant postmaster — and running her own household in a real house. She had come a long way from her brother's three-room cabin at Mountain Meadow Ranch. Alice still did much of the holiday preparations in the kitchen, but now domestic chores were shared with another.

"My chinaman brought me a present today, but I don't know whether it is to eat or to look at. It is like a huge lemon, about as large around as a quart bowl & nearly a foot tall. Hal is going to try to find out from one of the other chinamen what it is for. This one who comes here talks so little English I could not understand."

From this diary entry, it is obvious that Alice was more than puzzled, she was — to use a quaint word — discomfited.

"This one who comes here ..." The man must have had a name. Did Alice know it? Why didn't she use it?

Language wasn't the only invisible barrier that kept the lady from asking "her chinaman" about the strange fruit, herself. To do so would have meant admitting that he knew something she did not and would have placed that critical sense of position and propriety in jeopardy. That would not do; best to let her husband Hal handle the inquiries — somehow.

If Alice was puzzled about the nature of her gift, think how bizarre the Anglo-Saxon Christmas traditions must have seemed to Chinese immigrants who served in the community's households.

Emily Carr, a world-famous artist from BC, set down her memories of Christmas in *The Book of Small*: "We would all take hands and sing carols around the tree; Bong [the family's "chinaboy"] would come in and look with his mouth open," she writes. "There were always things on it [the tree] for him but he would not wait to get his presents. He would run back to his kitchen and we would take them to him there. It seemed as if Bong felt too Chinese to Christmas with us in our Canadian way."

Decades later, attitudes changed as immigrants' Canadian-born children grew up with the customs of Anglo-Saxon Christmas, yet still cherished the traditions of the country of their parents and grandparents.

Long-time BC resident Clare McAllister remembered the routine visits of what people of the time called the "vegetable Chinaman": "Just before Christmas, they brought us a box of lichee nuts, a box of ginger and a Chinese lily. We got the Chinese lily before Christmas, so we could get it ensconced in stones and water and it would bloom for New Year," Clare remembered. "It would be particularly nice if you had seven heads of blossoms on it because then you could tell old Wong and his pal, old Lee, that there were seven blossoms on the lily. This was viewed as very lucky."

Like hundreds of others, the Legace family moved west from Quebec to follow the work made possible by Canadian Pacific Railway construction. When the last rails were laid at the Vancouver terminus and the work was finished, the

Legaces stayed in British Columbia, and so did their French-Canadian customs. Peter Legace's parents settled near other French-speaking newcomers at Hatzic Prairie, in the Fraser Valley.

On Christmas Eve, the Legace family would attend mass, which would be held by the priest from the nearby community of Mission. It was a 16-kilometre carriage journey from Mission, and nobody was ever really sure when the priest would arrive.

"A couple of times he'd start up with George Rouleau ... and old Rouleau used to get drunk and it wasn't always sure when he'd bring the priest," recalled Peter, who was a young boy at the time. "It wasn't his fault. He'd get so full of booze. The old priest was too old to lift [Rouleau] into the carriage, so he walked the rest of the way. He'd get there at midnight or sometimes just about in time to have midnight mass. He'd come into our place and he'd be all in, you know. Well, we'd give him some tea and some coffee and a little drink of wine or something and he'd have to start to go to the church."

However, as the Legaces moved from one community to another, there wasn't always a church within easy travelling distance. That didn't stop the midnight mass. Others would gather at the Legace house. The priest would set up in the largest room and, as Peter recalled, "we'd have church at our place."

No large pipe organ. No stained-glass windows. No elaborate candelabras. Simply the celebration of Christmas, as it had been celebrated by the faithful for centuries, in song and prayer, in settings far more humble than that of the Legace household.

Chapter 2
Town and Country Christmases

 s the saying goes, there's no place like home for the holidays. In the late 19th century and early 20th century, "home" in British Columbia meant very different things to different people. For some of the province's early settlers, home was a bunkhouse in a coastal logging camp or on a Cariboo ranch. For others, it was a stately mansion on the slopes above bustling New Westminster or a small room in a modest working-class house in Victoria's James Bay. Regardless of where these early settlers were living, it seems most of them did what they could to ensure that the holidays were celebrated in some way.

Christmas On Burrard Inlet

By the 1880s, grand, granite-faced homes were being constructed not far from the brick hotels, bars, warehouses, and chandleries that now ringed Victoria's harbour. Across the Strait of Juan de Fuca, New Westminster's Columbia Street wharves and buildings hugged the Fraser River, and homes dotted the hills above the water's edge.

Things were very different on the heavily wooded shores of Burrard Inlet to the north. There was no rosy glow from gas lamps to light the way for a weary party of CPR surveyors. There were no comfortable carriages waiting to roll revellers down broad streets cobbled with wooden "bricks." No cheerful greetings shouted in the warm, congenial atmosphere of the bar on the corner for the numb, exhausted men who had been laying out the route of the transcontinental railway from Port Moody to Coal Harbour, at the edge of what is now Stanley Park. On Christmas Day 1884, there was merely the moan of the wind and the soft swish of snow pushed aside by stumbling feet, as the 15 men trudged through two-foot drifts.

Goaded on by the crusty, white-whiskered Major A.B. Rogers, the group pushed its way through stands of giant fir and cedar toward the tiny inlet mill settlement of Hastings, not far from today's Second Narrows Bridge.

For Major Rogers, this final part of his work for the new railroad was likely anti-climactic. He had risked life and limb in the Rockies in search of the best route — perhaps *any* route — to the coast. Given the nature of the day, it was likely that the men needed none of Rogers's usual blasphemous tirades to wrap up their work quickly and head for the warmth of what passed for civilization. Otway Wilkie was one of those men. Years later, he remembered that particular December 25.

"At the conclusion of the day's labour, just as it was getting dark, we reached a bluff of land about half a mile or more east of George Black's Brighton Hotel ... we all got into our boat, a large clinker-built boat about twenty feet long and capable of carrying twelve or fourteen men; no masts, just oars, which was on the beach, and made our way to Black's at Hastings where we celebrated Christmas dinner."

It was, as Wilkie described it, a "jolly party." Lonely loggers and mill-workers from Hastings and the neighbouring settlement of Moodyville had left their shacks to join the visiting surveyors. The men's revelry continued into the next cold, gray dawn.

Two years later, Christmas was celebrated in brand new hotels and buildings of what would become the city of Vancouver. A disastrous fire had levelled much of the town, but Granville, as it was then called, had "risen from the ashes." That was reason enough for celebration, but there was another reason for merriment that Christmas of 1886. The chief incentive for the rebuilding was the coming of the railroad. The burning question of which settlement — Port Moody or Granville — would be the terminus of the railroad had been settled by none other than the railroad's architect, William Van Horne. Van Horne had journeyed to the West Coast during the summer of 1884. Now, two years later, a newly constructed CPR wharf waited for the first trains. First, however, a very special free Christmas dinner awaited the CPR workers who had just finished the rail-line from Port Moody.

The city's future mayor, William Templeton, had ordered a ton of turkeys from Peterborough, Ontario, in honour of the occasion and as the community's expression of thanks for the hard-working railroad crews. The Methodist Church sponsored the free Christmas feast for the "navvies." Dan Campbell, Grandville's baker, slid 65 birds into his huge ovens for the Water Street banquet. A new city. A new railroad. They could see it coming, at last — urban civilization to rival Victoria and New Westminster.

A Cowboy's Christmas

Sometimes hundreds of kilometres away from the nearest large town, another type of community existed: the British Columbia cattle ranch. One of the largest was the Gang Ranch, a famous Cariboo spread. Just prior to World War I, the Gang Ranch not only boasted 7300 head of cattle, but its own sawmill and produce fields, too.

"There was an extremely friendly pioneer spirit about the Gang Ranch," remembered cowboy and rancher Harry Marriott. Because the ranch was far away from other settlements, it was a common occurrence that anybody travelling in the vicinity would call in as night fell. It was expected that visitors would stay over at the ranch to celebrate Christmas.

"I can remember a very, very fine Christmas at the Gang Ranch where everybody had a lot of rum and oh-be-joyful, you know, on Christmas Eve," Marriott reported. "Sometimes there were such big heads Christmas morning it was a hard matter to find boys to rustle around and feed any cattle that had to be fed."

After chores, there was Christmas dinner to look forward to.

"You got a damn good turkey dinner and they had a plum pudding and so on, on Christmas Day. Well, Christmas Eve, we're sitting around the bunkhouse and there comes a rattle-trap-slam-bang noise outside the door. I saw this thing going through the corral and a few minutes later, why, in staggers Fred Wycott. 'Well, boys, I'm flat broke now,' he says, 'but I'm home.'

"He was drunker than a hoot-owl," Harry remembered. "He'd gone through nine thousand bucks that summer."

Nevertheless, Fred was "home." And, according to Harry, when he came home, like so many others, Fred had a job automatically with the Gang Ranch, Christmastime — or any time — "he showed up."

A Christmas Comedy
Smithers, British Columbia, was by no means a large

community in the early 1900s, but it offered its residents all the amenities. The town had three or four paved streets and a few real electric streetlights, courtesy of local entrepreneur W. J. "Wiggs" O'Neil, who operated a small electrical plant. It also had brick-fronted specialty shops — men's wear, ladies' wear, hardware, barbershops, a restaurant or two, a bank, and a drugstore. Indeed, it seemed that by 1913, Smithers had it all. It was enough to make people think carefully before making that long trip to Prince George to do their Christmas shopping.

As Christmas Day approached, the enterprising Wiggs O'Neil worked hard at putting the finishing touches on an attraction that he — and others — were sure would put Smithers on the map. There, on the corner of Main Street and Fourth Avenue, stood O'Neil's brand new movie house, the only one around for hundreds of kilometres. Crossing his fingers, he set the date of the grand opening for Christmas Eve.

On the appointed day, an eager crowd gathered out front, then filed inside and waited in anticipation for the lights to dim and the silent, black and white images to hit the screen. A few minutes later, the audience was sitting patiently in the dark, but no images lit up the screen. For some reason, the projector simply wouldn't project.

Frustrated and embarrassed, O'Neil gave his patrons back their tickets and asked them to return after Christmas dinner the following night, and they would "give it another try." The next night, after turkey and dressing, the people of

Smithers dutifully did exactly that.

"People were really tolerant, in those days," O'Neil remembered. Most likely, the real incentive to return was the opportunity for a novel Christmas experience which was, most certainly, a first-time experience for many of those who bought tickets the night before. Besides, what was there to do back home? A card game or singing around the piano — you could do that any time — paled in comparison to the chance to experience this new marvel of the modern age. The equipment worked wonderfully. However, by the following holiday season, nothing in the theatre was working at all. It was dark and empty, its doors locked.

It seemed that Christmas 1914 would be a bleak one. There was a war on. And, as Wiggs recalled, "everyone was broke, or close to it." Business was bad. The movie theatre closed. Yet, more than ever, people needed a reason to laugh. Someone suggested to O'Neil that he send out for a film and run a show at Christmas, just to cheer the townspeople up. O'Neil got on the phone and ordered a two-reel comedy and a feature comedy. He didn't care what it was, as long as it was funny.

Other plans were underway. One of the few couples who had enjoyed a decent business that year were the Fatherbys. Hudson was a blacksmith, and his wife ran a boarding house and restaurant. The couple, O'Neil said, "decided to put on a swank Christmas turkey dinner. Invitations were sent out and it was the talk of the town for a week." Not all the talk was likely positive. "For some reason, he invited no one that didn't belong to the top crust of the town. The druggist and his lady, the Union Bank manager, the Buckley Hotel manager and his lady, the Grand Trunk Pacific superintendent and some others whom one might call our elite set." It is easy to guess the motivation for the inclusion of those on the guest list. Hudson and his wife had a lot to be thankful for, and undoubtedly knew who it would be most advantageous to thank.

As the night proceeded, flushed with the success of the dinner, Hudson Fatherby, no doubt stroking his large black moustache, expansively invited all his diners to the picture show — on him!

Inside the theatre, everything was going off without a hitch. Everyone was having a wonderful time — upper crust and lower class alike. The lights came on as the reels were changed. Now, it was time for the feature. O'Neil had promised a "comedy" — he didn't specify what movie it was. Nobody did. This was long before "movie stars" or revered film directors. "Christmas Day movies" was all the townspeople needed to know. Or so they thought.

The lights went down, the projector whirred, and there, on the screen, was the title of the feature: *Blacksmith Breaks Into Society.*

Wiggs was mortified.

"I was nearly floored when I saw it, but what could one do?" Laugh, most likely, as people in the audience were already starting to do. It got worse — or better, depending on your point of view and status within the community.

"As the picture unfolded, it showed the blacksmith with a huge black moustache, very much resembling Hudson," O'Neil recounted 40 years later. "He tucked his napkin into his shirt collar, shovelled the food in with his knife, tried to balance peas on his knife and wound up by drinking the finger-bowl dry, lemon and all."

Any movie was bound to be a welcome attraction, but this one was an unqualified hit. O'Neil was relieved to learn that among those who laughed the loudest, "until the tears ran down his cheeks" was the Smithers blacksmith himself.

When the movie ended, the laughter continued out in the lobby.

"Some called me the incorrigible Wiggs, and accused me of pulling a put-up job because I had not been invited to dinner," O'Neil recalled. "But all I can say is, it was one of those rare things that just happened. I was as innocent as a babe."

Maybe.

Bulkley Valley Christmas Party

Christmas has always been a time for gathering together with friends and family. Like many British Columbians today, those who populated the province in the past often travelled out of their way to be with others. It often took them days to reach the homes of far-flung neighbours or family members, people they saw very rarely the rest of the year.

Somehow, despite the distances that separated the province's early settlers from one another, word would get out — by dogsled, stagecoach, telegraph, bicycle, or word-of-mouth — when a Christmas gathering was planned.

In 1915, Sarah "Nan" Bourgon and her friends began to organize a Christmas party for the growing community of Bulkley Valley. They sat and planned who to invite. "We've quite a few people in [the area] now," commented one of Nan's friends, thinking about people scattered over the countryside. "There's a couple up there, they have two little children. They look so lonesome ..."

As the party preparations continued, the friends settled on a place to hold their festive gathering. "Now, a French-Canadian named Billy Fidel put up a hotel," Nan remembered years later, "and I believe if you had gone and pushed against it, you'd push the damn thing over. It was that ramshackle ... So we went over and we looked at Billy Fidel's place. Well, the cracks in it were like all the rest of the places. You could shoot peas through the cracks."

In spite of its ramshackle condition, Billy's hotel was voted the designated party place. Further plans were made. Chickens were substituted for hard-to-find turkeys, and the women prepared mouth-watering mince pieces, plum puddings, and cakes. "They brought in the most gorgeous cakes," Nan recalled. "One of them was a huge chocolate cake, oh, about a four layer ... we stuck it in the centre of the big table in the kitchen."

Meanwhile, the men brought the small church organ into the hotel, and soon the hotel was filled with music and singing. The party went on and on. When the Fidel children grew tired, their mother put them to bed upstairs.

Then, in the wee hours, the revellers decided to raid the leftovers before starting for home. Into the kitchen they trooped. "When we got in there," Nan recounted, "these kids — there were no rubber pants in those days — these two darn kids had wet [the bed upstairs] and it had gone all through the middle of the chocolate cake! Then all of a sudden I laughed, and we all laughed. The part that amused me was all us women, when we saw these drips still dripping, you know, picking things up and running around — we had no place to put them. The only place we could put them was on the stairs. Then we all had one good big laugh ... That was our Christmas. It was the first one that we ever had in the Bulkley Valley. And I venture to say it was the best one, too."

Big City Christmases

The tragic legacy of World War I — a brother killed, the fearful ravages of disease, a father felled by influenza immediately following the armistice — hit Clare McAllister's family hard. Realizing they needed a new start, the McAllisters left Nelson for New Westminster. Clare was a high school student by then, and the vibrant urban environment of BC's Royal City was just the distraction she needed to put the grief behind her.

Among Clare's many exciting discoveries was shopping — real shopping. "I'm thinking of the stores at Christmastime," Clare smiled, warming to her memories. "There weren't as many stores up on the hills as there are now. They were all down below, near the [Fraser] river." And if the shops and stores on Columbia Street weren't enough, "one went over to Vancouver to the larger stores to do some shopping. One went from New Westminster to Vancouver on the old BC Electric inter-urban tram, with its many way stations. Thrifty people didn't buy a 35-cent through-ticket from the depot in New Westminster. There was something called settlers' tickets, and you bought one from New Westminster to wherever it was — in the middle of Burnaby — and then a ticket from there through to Vancouver; you had books of these, and this maybe gave you a trip for 27 cents instead of 35 cents."

The trip through "dark Burnaby," as Clare remembered it, was "full of woods and lakes and the little way stations, then you got off ... and had to transfer onto a streetcar on the Vancouver streetcar system."

What a reversal! Less than 50 years before, traffic had all gone the other way. In the 1870s, before the CPR tracks made their way down Burrard Inlet, it was New Westminster, on the Fraser River — a busy river ever since the gold rush — that was the height of urban sophistication on the mainland.

Those bound for a family Christmas in New Westminster bought tickets for the steamer passage from the coal port of Nanaimo or Victoria, crossed their fingers, and hoped the mouth of the Fraser would remain navigable.

The Fraser River would ice up and, confound the luck, the steamer would be forced to go up through Burrard Narrows to dock at Hastings — there was absolutely no alternative — and passengers would disembark, climb into a stagecoach, and endure the overland trip to New Westminster.

But for Clare McAllister, all this was ancient history. This was the 1920s, after all, an era of trains, trams, and cars that sped newly affluent shoppers to Woolworth's and the Hudson's Bay and Woodward's department stores.

"They would be so jammed near Christmas that you would literally have to fight and push your way around the aisles," Clare recalled. "Christmas didn't set up so early as it does now, with the merchants advertising, and therefore, there was more of a rush to get the shopping done all at one time."

Certain Christmas shopping details made a lasting impression on the young woman from the Interior. Among the top fashions of the day were ladies' kid gloves, a must-have item for the high society set. "Certain people who live up in Shaughnessy would be looking forward to balls at the Hotel Vancouver, no doubt. You would see ladies at the glove counter, where there were little satin cushions on which people rested an elbow and held up a left hand. The clerk would inquire the size of the glove. You would see the clerk carefully working the fingers of the kid gloves down the [fingers] of the lady's hand."

Candy department, David Spencer Ltd., Vancouver

Lingerie of the time was of genuine silk, Clare recalled, some hand-embroidered Chinese crèpe and see-through crèpe de Chine and chiffon. And, for $125, the discerning shopper could purchase a top-quality muskrat fur coat.

In 1926, Vancouver Christmas shoppers had a brand new destination, a nine-storey building at the corner of Hastings and Richards Streets, the latest addition to the merchantile empire of David Spencer. What you couldn't see, as you walked down the sidewalk, were the five storeys that existed below street level. Shoppers had a total of 320,000 square feet of browsing and buying opportunities.

Spencer's had no grocery department, as Eaton's was to have, but it did have something else that Clare McAllister found much more fascinating. "They had the extraordinary entertainment of a man who made tarts in a window that would have been facing the CPR station. He did it by cutting off uniform dollops of pastry and hurling them rapidly into the tart pans." The pastry artist pounded the pastry with an iron heated in a gas flame so that they would instantaneously assume the shape of the fluted cups.

As wonderful as Spencer's merchandise was, it was more than equaled by the building itself — a far cry from the rectangular, non-descript big-box stores shoppers hurry into today. Spencer's combined convenience with a "beautiful façade which gives character and strength to the building," the *Morning Star* reported on December 10, "... handsome arcade and show-windows."

"The particular thing that was glorious about it was marble floor brought from Italy," Clare recalled. It was beautiful, but not too practical, in Clare's view, as the porous marble tended to trap dirt. A small price to pay, perhaps, for the beauty of it all.

Other must-see attractions were the Christmas decorations inside Birk's Jewellers, where cedar boughs were twined around the elegant staircase and holly festooned windows and countertops. Outside, streetlights and lampposts were decorated with genuine cedar and holly. In an era before the

Christmas decorations of David Spencer Ltd., Victoria, 1929

introduction of traffic lights, uniformed policemen directed busy holiday traffic.

"The policeman at the corner of Georgia and Granville, standing in the middle of the street, would have boxes and boxes of gifts piled around his feet," Clare remembered. When shoppers stepped into an elevator, white-gloved operators closed metal doors, tilted levers, and melodiously announced the merchandise to be found on each approaching floor. Clare McAllister recalled that Christmastime was a time of generosity towards these tireless workers. "Elevator

48

girls would have boxes and boxes of chocolates," she added, in recalling those long-ago shopping days.

City folks paused in their shopping excursions to enjoy special events and entertainment.

As the holiday season approached, the tempo of Vancouver's nightlife quickened, as countless businesses booked their once-a-year Christmas parties. What might begin in an office after closing time, would continue in one of the large dance halls, the Winter Gardens, perhaps, which was built on a pier that extended out over the West End waters. Inside hotels, such as the Devonshire, couples danced under enormous brightly coloured paper bells. In 1921, at the original Hotel Vancouver, over 70 guests in their formal finery enjoyed the gala Christmas party hosted by the Orpheum Theatre.

Clare McAllister had her own special Christmas memories of that Vancouver theatrical landmark located next to the original Hotel Vancouver. As a student at the University of British Columbia, she joined hundreds of others in the dash for 50-cent gallery tickets to look down on Christmas stage productions from the topmost theatre level.

"There we saw such things as Gilbert and Sullivan, we saw the Stratford-On-Avon players doing Shakespeare and I saw Pavlova (the famous ballerina) dance, in Vancouver. I knew nothing about ballet ... and I can well remember the absolutely blazing kind of incredulity with which I saw her ... dance the dying swan from Swan Lake. Her hands flutteredlikewingsandshewentdownanddownanddownand down to infinite degrees, slowly, with the spotlight, of course, on her."

Chapter 3
Tree and Turkey

mong the most-loved activities of the Christmas season are trimming the tree and feasting on holiday treats. For more than a century, both the Christmas tree and Christmas dinner have served as warm, welcoming symbols of holiday merriment and togetherness.

An Enduring, Adaptable Tradition
Since the 1840s, the Christmas tree has been an enduring focal point of Christmas celebrations. In fact, in many instances, this green and living Yuletide tradition has often given its very name to a particular event or celebration, as it did in the Vernon area in 1896. As Alice Parke recorded in her diary, "the Christmas tree" was well worth making the trip

into town by cutter (a large open sleigh) from the BX Ranch where her husband, Hal, was the manager: "We went in to the Presbyterian Xmas Tree last night. A whole load from here went — all except Furniss and Orr. Orr came over & kept house for us. Hal asked him to have the kettle boiling, so when we got home from the tree I made a cup of coffee and we had coffee, cake and apples ..."

As times and circumstances changed, the ever-adaptable Christmas tree has been there, to conveniently serve and promote special, timely needs. In Nelson, and perhaps in dozens of other British Columbia communities, the Christmas tree became a symbol of support for thousands of men in uniform and their families back home, during times of war.

On December 15, 1916, the *Nelson Daily News* reported: "All a-glitter to its topmost peak which reached away up into the skylight. In Eagle Hall, a huge Christmas tree was provided by the women of Nelson for the kiddies whose names are on the District Patriotic Fund Lists. The Festive tree delighted 125 youngsters' hearts yesterday afternoon and Old St. Nicholas himself attended, and distributed parcels and good things."

Today, the "tree" often comes out of a box and is quickly assembled. In early days, the tree, likely as not, came out of a forest, no assembly necessary. Decades later, the former acts of searching for, selecting, and cutting down the tree became fond and cherished memories. For Clare McAllister,

Christmas tree decorations, Victoria, c. 1918

the Christmas trees of her turn-of-the-century childhood in Nelson left an indelible mark upon her memory.

"The particular thing about Christmas in those days was the smell of Christmas," Clare remarked. Nelson, like so many British Columbia communities, was small. The town was surrounded by forest. Clare remembered nostalgically that, "all the trees were fresh cut, so that when the tree came ... out of the frosty, snowy winter air, into a warm house, it smelled of Christmas."

Emily Carr knew exactly what Clare meant. "Just before Christmas we went out into the woods and cut down a fir tree and brought it home still so alive that the warm house fooled it into thinking spring had come and it breathed delicious live pine smell all over the house," she wrote in *The Book of Small.*

First Chopping, Then Shopping

Obtaining a live Christmas tree was a true Christmas adventure. It was a special occasion, not, as it often is today, simply another complication to be jammed in on the hurried commute from work or while dashing into a big-box retailer for an extra set of lights.

Major J.S. Matthews, the founder of Vancouver City Archives, placed enough importance on the cultural rituals surrounding the Christmas tree that he left details of Christmas tree excursions behind for future generations. Labelling his reminiscences "A cursory memorandum before I forget," he wrote:

"There was no Christmas tree problem before the Great War; it was more a matter of 'where should we go to get one?' Those who had horse and buggy found it easy; others took the streetcar. Frequently, school boys called, usually at the front door, either with a small fir tree they had cut somewhere, or 'getting orders' as they called it. And their price ranged from twenty-five cents up to as much as one dollar; often their childish limit was the 'immense' sum of ten cents for something very scraggly they had dragged a long way.

"The more fortunate, who lived in Hastings, Grandview, Mt. Pleasant, South Vancouver, the new Shaughnessy or Kitsilano, simply went out in the clearing and cut one; it was a little trouble; the weather may be inclement, but there was some fun about it; to go with the children — next Saturday afternoon, or Sunday morning when Father was not at work — and get Mother a Christmas tree; large or small, as she wished.

"But one day, I recall the first occasion, when, at Kitsilano Beach, we took a small axe and started off, with the children, to cut a Christmas tree in the Indian Reserve. We came back with empty hands; we could not find one; they had all gone. That was about 1913."

By then, tracts of wooded land were marked out for roads and residential lots. What was once rural was now urban. Nevertheless, where there is a need, there will be those ready to fill it.

"After the war [World War I], and about Christmas 1918 or a year or so later, there were men who went out and gathered Christmas trees; just one or two, and, if memory serves correctly, the first I saw was a man who had a few stacked together on what was afterwards called, 'Victory Square,' but

David Miller on the "Sea Queen" brings home a
Christmas tree from Discovery Island, Victoria,
December 18, 1938

before the Cenotaph was erected." The man was clever: the
street traffic in that part of downtown would have been heavy,
even then. "He had a few [trees] for sale, and later, perhaps
the same year, was to experience competition." Obviously,
others recognized a good thing when they saw it.

At the start of the Depression, competition for a good
location — and the extra income that you simply had to have

to buy a few Christmas presents and a turkey — became fierce. "The street-corner Christmas tree trade developed until, about 1935, or so, men contested for street-corners; some started earlier than others; some said they had held a certain corner for years, and when another man 'jumped' his corner, there was a squabble; even a fight, and the police were called to allay the disturbance."

So much for the "season of goodwill." Then things changed, yet again. In late November 1939, Major Matthews was walking up the hill toward Vancouver city hall when he noticed a group of about 30 men waiting patiently in the rain beneath the steps of the building's north entrance. He walked up to one of the men and asked him what was going on.

"His reply astonished me," the major remembered. The man said they were lined up to get permits to sell Christmas trees.

A Very Magical Thing

"Christmas then was utterly unlike Christmas now," Clare McAllister said as she reminisced about years gone by. "Of course, all old people think their kind of Christmas was better ... the Christmas tree was not put up weeks before, it was erected, magically, on Christmas Eve by Santa Claus. On Christmas night, of course, the candles would be lit, and there is nothing more magical than a living room fireplace blazing and the candles in a dim room on a lighted tree; it's a very magical thing."

Duke Ackerman recalled the magic, too, in the living room of his family's small James Bay home. "Well, you know, no electric lights, ever. I remember the house on Lewis Street, for years when I was a kid we never had no electric lights at all. Candles; Christmas candles. Little red ones. I saw them clip them on the branches."

And this, in an era before smoke detectors, fire extinguishers, and "fire retardant" synthetic trees! "If you had to go out," Ackerman explained, "you wouldn't leave them on all night. You'd blow them out. There was always somebody in the house. You never had no more fires than you have now. A lot of these fires are just carelessness," he scoffed.

Clare McAllister was of the same opinion: "People perish at the thought of candles on a Christmas tree, but I never heard of any Christmas tree going on fire like I have with electric lights," she laughed. "People took great care to put the candles nice and steady in their little nippers that clutched the branches and they didn't put them immediately under another branch."

As the years went by, those candles were supplanted by electric lights. If those old white or red candles were taken out of the boxes from the attic or basement, they were clipped to branches merely as remembrances of Christmases past, rarely to be lighted again.

Electric lights were difficult to obtain during the World War II years, but by the late 1940s, they were back with a vengeance, led by a brand new innovation. As Christmas tree ornament-makers had discovered decades before, it wasn't enough simply to have an ornament that glimmered and gleamed. Motion made the difference. The newest incarnation in those early post-war years was the "bubble light." Long, thin glass tubes, holding coloured liquid, protruded from a coloured plastic bulb. When plugged in, the heat from the light inside the bulb warmed the liquid, which bubbled merrily up the length of the tube. Each year, as the angel and glass balls were unpacked, as the tinsel was untangled, the bubble light fascinated and delighted children of a new generation long into the 1950s, in the same way that Mickey Mouse lights had charmed their parents in their childhood decades before.

Sophisticated Dining
Traditional Christmas dinners are always a sight to behold. Laid out on fine tablecloths are dishes filled with Brussels sprouts, carrots, turnips, broccoli, mashed potatoes, cranberry sauce, and stuffing. And then, of course, there is the turkey, which is carved at the table, or served, steaming, on large platters. This is the meal that countless families in British Columbia have enjoyed for years and years on Christmas Day.

But picture this for Christmas dinner: oysters on the half shell and chicken bisque, followed by baked stuffed salmon, delicious lobster, and banana fritters with vanilla sauce. Next, "stuffed young" turkey, loin of pork, tamed goose, duck, sirloin of beef, as well as lemon snow pudding and custard sauce.

In what fine establishment could a hungry patron find such a sophisticated feast? Not the Vancouver Hotel, or any of the up-scale restaurants on Granville Street; not inside Victoria's Empress Hotel, or even across the street at the Union Club. Instead, this was the dinner offered to patrons of the Kalamalka Hotel on Barnard Avenue, in Vernon, in 1925.

"A Real Christmas Dinner without the trouble of cooking at home," the headline of the hotel's newspaper advertisement enthused. In 1925, the hard-working folks at the north end of the lake might have been a little "rough around the edges" compared to the big city folks on the coast, but they knew how to do it up in style — if they could afford to. The cost of the Christmas dinner at the Kalamalka was one dollar per plate, but that didn't seem to deter the good people of Vernon. Small wonder the ad advised making "your reservations early. Phone 24."

Throughout British Columbia, there were other special dinners associated with the Yuletide season. In Nelson, there were "game suppers" held before Christmas. "These were for the gentlemen only," long-time Nelson resident Clare McAllister later recalled, "and you would have everything from bear, mountain goat, venison, grouse, trout, salmon, char, sturgeon ... a great mass of protein."

But that wasn't all.

"A distinction of festive meals in those times was the

Preparations for dinner in a Vancouver home, c. 1900

incredible number of desserts," Clare continued. "You had white Christmas cake, dark Christmas cake, mince pie, plum pudding, and sherbet cups of jelly with whipped cream on top, and heaven help you if you did not consume at least a mouthful of all these kinds of sweets that came at the end of the meal."

Culinary Creativity
Christmases in the early 1900s were a time for men to relax and for women to work. Usually, women would spend

countless hours preparing meals and desserts for their large families. "My grandmother used to make all the Christmas puddings and all the cakes," Duke Ackerman remembered fondly. "Everything was homemade. You didn't go in a shop in them days, you made it yourself. The house was full at Christmas. In my mother's family, there were 11, and they had sons and daughters and everything; it was a big affair, coming around the house every Christmas."

Emily Carr particularly recalled the plum puddings of her childhood Christmases. In *The Book Of Small,* she nostalgically wrote, "Plum puddings were dangling from under the pantry shelf by the tails of their boiling cloths. A month ago we had all sat round the breakfast-room table, stoning raisins while someone read a story aloud. Everyone had given the pudding a good-luck stir before it went into the bowls and was tied down and boiled for hours in the copper wash boiler while spicy smells ran all over the house. On Christmas Day, the biggest pudding came out for a final boil before being brought to the table with brandy fire leaping up its sides from the dish and with a sprig of holly scorching and crackling on its top."

Doris Smith, who grew up in Revelstoke in the early 1900s, remembers how hard her mother worked during the Christmas season and how her father couldn't even perform the task of carving the turkey. "Christmas was more for the men," she stated rather bluntly, recalling the Christmases when the men of the neighbourhood took things a little too far. "I don't know how, one must have started it ... [the men would] go to somebody's house and this man would join them and they'd go to the next house. By the time it was two or three in the afternoon, there would be about a dozen men and they'd come and call at the house and there was always hot drinks or Tom and Jerry's ...

"Mother had to stay home and cook the turkey, which was then, of course, *not* enjoyed by the head of the household." Doris laughed at the memory. "He felt no pain, then, you see. He didn't care for his dinner. I remember that so well because we had many a Christmas dinner spoiled."

A Turkey By Any Other Name...
In British Columbia's pioneer days, turkey and goose were not always the main entrees at Christmas dinner. While chicken and duck were often worthy substitutes, some early settlers were forced to come up with more original alternatives.

Among the settlers in the Chilcotin were "Bunch" Trudeau and her father. One year, 18 bachelors came from near and far to enjoy Christmas dinner at the Trudeaus' log cabin. Bunch's father had taught his daughter cooking. That Christmas, she prepared an elaborate, but mysterious feast.

"They all came for supper and we had roast of bear — of course, we never told them it was bear — and we had a roast of goat and a roast of deer." Bunch recalled the dinner included stuffed potatoes, vegetables, and "pies of all descriptions." The bear meat went unnamed, but not unnoticed. Guests ate most of the goat, a little of the venison, but by meal's end, the bear meat had completely disappeared.

Two or three weeks after the holiday, on the regularly scheduled mail day, their Christmas guests returned to the cabin to pick up parcels and letters. Bunch's father decided to have a little fun.

"Daddy brought the conversation around, as he could, to eating bear meat. Oh, there were some that wouldn't eat bear, no sir, you couldn't get them to eat bear, and at last, Daddy quietly told them, 'Oh, I think you've eaten bear.' 'No, I've never eaten bear,' you know, and, 'Oh, I think you have, in fact,' Daddy says, 'I know you have. At Christmas dinner.'

"Do you know that three of them went outside and were sick and they just still couldn't take it, and yet it was really awfully good bear, and it was just done to a turn, just nice and crisp. It was just like pork, really. Maybe they figured it was pork, but I don't know where in the world they ever thought we got pigs."

Joyeux Noel

Around the same time the *mikan* made its first appearance in Victoria, another kind of Christmas ritual was being established at Hatzic Prairie in the Fraser Valley. Every year, about a week before Christmas, Peter Legace's mother would start to make French meat pies, a French-Canadian tradition.

"Our mother used to make pork pies, mince pies. We'd make our own mince meat and used to always make a

50-pound tub of that, using the necks of the beef."

This was a culinary art that Mrs. Legace brought from her native Quebec when the Legace family moved west with the CPR. Christmas meals in the Legaces' Fraser Valley household were always special. "Mother always used to have brandy, and she blew the light out, and we finished the dinner when the dessert came, with candles, and then they would bring in the pudding, set it afire ... You'd have two or three of them, light them in the kitchen and then bring them in with that blue flame."

While the menu items varied with the time, place, and custom, the common thread woven through these and countless other Christmas dinners was the camaraderie and spirit of festive celebration that this once-a-year meal, whatever its particular dishes, signified to all those who sat around the table.

Chapter 4
Here Comes Santa Claus

very year, children across Canada go to bed on Christmas Eve eagerly anticipating a visit from Santa Claus. With their eyes squeezed shut and their spirits hopeful, they wait for the jolly man in the red suit to slide down the chimney and leave gifts for them under the tree. Most spend the weeks leading up to Christmas preparing for this most important of visits. They comb through catalogues and race through toy stores, eyes peeled for the perfect gift to ask for from Santa. Acting on their best behaviour, they visit his look-alikes at nearby shopping malls and department stores. Those who do not

have access to one of Santa's helpers might chose instead to write a letter to the man himself, detailing the gift or gifts they would like to receive. This eager anticipation of Santa's visit, this build-up of excitement, has been present in British Columbia for well over a century.

A Children's Paradise

Vancouver's brand new Spencer's department store seemed to offer so much for everyone during the 1926 gift-giving season. An intriguing inclusion in the Spencer's promotional supplement to the *Morning Star* two weeks before Christmas read: "... and, Spencer's toyland offers a paradise for children."

During an era when department stores (Eatons, The Bay, Simpson-Sears, Woodward's and Spencer's) reigned supreme, these national or regional retail powerhouses generated a Christmastime merchandising momentum that built relentlessly over the ensuring decades, through war and peace, good times and bad. During the free-spending 1920s, so great was the competition for parents' Christmas present cash among the major department stores, it ushered in what was to become an annual phenomenon: the noisy, colourful world of the toyland. By the fabulous (and affluent) 1950s, department store toylands had reached a pinnacle of consumer Yuletide experience, and, some would argue, promotional excess. What is often forgotten, however, is that until the latter part of the 20th century, customers didn't simply come to buy and hurry away again. They came with their children, to watch, to marvel, and to dream.

At the beginning of every season, on the very floor space where, just days before, the linen department or the housewares department had existed, there arose, overnight, a special, magical world of marvelous toys, surrounded by painted castle walls and a formal "drawbridge" entrance that led children to — yes! There he was! — Santa Claus. Santa held court for visiting children from his elevated chair (sometimes suspiciously resembling a royal throne), ably assisted by costumed female "elves" or even Mrs. Claus. As they do today in shopping malls, children would approach with reverence — and sometimes fear — to sit on his knee and say what they would like under the tree. From inside a small wooden structure camouflaged as some fantasy castle, flashbulbs would burst, and a photographic keepsake of little Donny or Daphne would be ready to take home in its "Merry Christmas" paper folder, to be wedged into the triangular black corners licked down into place on a new page of the family photo album.

The advent of television made it possible for manufacturers to demonstrate toys right there in the living rooms of the nation. It took 20 years for toy-makers to really catch on, but by the swinging '60s, beginning with preschool programs such as *Romper Room*, the medium began to pitch a myriad of must-have toys, from Barbie dolls and Hot Wheels to G.I. Joe and My Little Pony.

Prior to the 1960s, however, toy-makers could really only market their Christmas product lines two ways: through department store Christmas catalogues and the department store toyland. Of course, toylands weren't really for kids at all, nor even for their parents. Toylands were really designed for toy-makers. Because kids and their parents could actually touch the toys, and watch them work, the toyland was by far the most effective opportunity for toy-makers to market those precious goods. For the toy manufacturer or distributor, Christmastime in Toyland was "make or break" time.

So, unlike today's retail toy area, in which boxes of merchandise are simply stacked statically on massive metal shelving, between the 1920s and 1960s, toylands were alive with sound and motion. If you were under 12 and primed for it all weeks before by the colourful pages of the Eaton's or Simpson-Sears catalogues, the anticipation almost drove you mad. If you were a mom or a dad, the excitement was contagious. The print ads goaded parents by the millions to bundle up their kids and climb aboard streetcars, buses, or, later, jump into the family's first car, and head downtown, destination: Toyland!

Dolls tottered across tabletops and cried "ma-ma" while wind-up locomotives chugged around on the circles of track, or electric trains raced in and out of mountain tunnels and through miniature towns; little red balls bounced off Bollo Bats; firetrucks rolled down aisles with miniature lights flashing and sirens screaming; steam shovels lifted and dropped dirt; Slinkies slinked; Roy Rogers cap six-shooters snapped and popped; Daisy Air Rifles cracked and smoked. Kids — and not a few dads — stood goggle-eyed as experts painstakingly constructed amazing Meccano machines. "Come back tomorrow," they would say, "and see how far we've got!"

Even the static displays were eye-popping: rows of intricate tinker-toy creatures were arrayed around their cylindrical cardboard containers. A British Models' "thin red line" of pith-helmeted lead soldiers, rifles at the ready, knelt and stood resolutely in the face of charging scimitar-wielding Arabs on horseback, while, nearby, the band of Her Majesty's Royal Marines staged a march-past.

Representatives and store employees spent hours twisting keys, pushing or pulling wheeled things made of cast-iron, wood, tin, bakelite, and later, high-impact plastic. Others furnished dollhouses, wound up the elastic bands of airplane propellers, or changed doll diapers. And, all the while, in spite of aching feet, they kept smiling, smiling, smiling.

Then came Christmas morning.

Inside the red felt Christmas stocking, heavy and bulging with promise: a Hopalong Cassidy Little Big Book, a miniature plastic game, bubble solution or a white lacrosse ball, homemade doll clothes for the doll under the tree, a small net-bag of marbles (cat's eyes, peeries and cobbs), a Dinky Toy army jeep, a package of baseball cards with that never-to-be forgotten scent of sweet-smelling gum, a porcelain Triceratops or Tyrannosaurus Rex, a kazoo or shiny silver whistle, wax lips, licorice pipes and candy cigarettes, a plastic ring, a skipping rope, Viewmaster reels of Little Lulu or the Lone Ranger, a set of jacks — marvelous stuff.

Nothing — and Everything — from Santa

Bad behaviour meant that Bert Williams and his brothers and sisters wouldn't find anything on Christmas morning, or so their parents told them. When the big day came, there was evidence that Santa had, indeed, paid a visit: all that was left of the cake the kids had left out for him was a few scattered crumbs on an empty plate. One look in the stockings, however, turned Christmas morning anticipation to abject disappointment. The stockings weren't filled with toys, they were filled with wood-shavings!

"Well, I declare," Bert Williams said as he recounted this tragic Christmas tale, "he [Santa] was getting a calling down, I'll tell you, about how mean he was, and all this sort of thing. We wouldn't be good. We wouldn't be good anymore! We wasn't gonna be!"

It didn't matter what day it was, when you were a member of a Langley farm family, there were chores to be done. Hop to it, his parents said. Bert stomped out to the stable to feed the horses.

"There's a hay loft overhead ... hanging from the ceiling, there was the biggest Christmas tree you ever saw, and it was absolutely loaded. Well, of course, down I went to the house and my eyes were sticking out like saucers and I couldn't talk plain or tell them what it was. I remember that year I got a mouth-organ and an axe. My brother got an axe and a little gun. And other things, candies and things, all tied up. Wonderful presents."

In later years, that fondly remembered Christmas seemed even more miraculous when Bert understood the special efforts his parents had made. Gift-giving wasn't as simple as going to a department store or ordering items from a catalogue. Mr. Williams packed those presents home on his back, and it wasn't a short walk, either. It was a long, arduous journey by foot and ferry to New Westminster. Making the journey down to the Royal City was the easy part. Coming back was much more difficult. Once off the ferry, it was an eight-kilometre hike through the bush with those awkward, heavy parcels.

As children do, there were sly comparisons made later on that day and in the days that followed. "Some of the richer kids had better [gifts] and nicer shoes or something like that," Bert said, "but we were always satisfied, and it was a wonderful time."

Up in Nelson, Clare McAllister was, she later realized, exactly what Bert and his buddies would have called a "richer kid." With the clear-eyed vision that comes with maturity, Clare came to understand that her childhood Christmases in Nelson were truly "upper class" Christmases, the kind enjoyed by the families of the judges, doctors, lawyers, and CPR executives. Clare's own father, M.R. McQuarrie, was a successful real estate agent who would also become mayor.

"A child went down from a stocking on the bedpost ... in my ruinously spoiled state, I also had another Christmas stocking hanging by the fireplace. Perhaps this was just to keep me quiet in the morning. There was always a piece of coal and a Japanese orange in the toe of the stocking."

More than one pioneer mentions the "lump of coal," usually in disparaging terms. However what most had forgotten — or never understood — was that the coal was once a good luck token. In any case, Clare's orange was quickly eaten, and then it was downstairs to unwrap presents. On this particular Christmas, World War I was in its third year. "In the patriotic spirit ... there was a large box of chocolates with the British flag spread out on it," Clare recalled. There was "a gift from a family friend — many hours of painstaking work — a heavy cotton nightgown embroidered with pink scallops, pink ribbons, and with it, something known as a boudoir cap, which I think was thing that ladies pulled on over their hair when it was done up with kit curlers ... it was something, I suppose, to make a small girl think that she was getting to be a lady. Young ladies carried their dancing slippers in a satin bag with a silk cord. I was given one of these."

The Letter to Santa
The Tatangelos, and other Italians living in Trail, called it *spaniolla*. Most other people called it "the flu." In any case, it was the 20th century scourge that authorities are only now

recognizing as one of the worst epidemics of any century, anywhere. Giuseppe Tatangelo was a husband, father, and one of Trail's tireless community volunteers. When the epidemic claimed him just a week before Christmas, it was the hardest death of three that had crushed the family since they had immigrated to the Kootenays nine years before. First, four-year-old Enrico had drowned in a rain barrel. Then, five years later, little two-year-old Peter had succumbed to a rare illness.

Now, while other households in the mining community prepared for the festive season, Pasqua, the Tatangelo children's mother, was inconsolable in her loss. To take the children's minds off the tragedy, one of their uncles suggested they should all write a letter to Santa Claus.

Eight-year-old Enrico (named to commemorate his deceased brother) finished his letter and carefully placed it in the oven. Why not? That way, it would be magically whisked up the chimney to Santa. Six-year-old Mary thought she knew better. She was adamant she was going to mail her letter to the North Pole, and so off to the post office she went. The postmaster noticed the address on the letter. Of course, in the small, tightly knit community, the latest Tatangelo tragedy was on everyone's lips. The postmaster took the liberty of opening up Mary's letter.

A few days before Christmas, Mary found a little note in the Tatangelo mailbox addressed to her. The note asked her to please come to the post office on Christmas morning. The date did not surprise her: in those days the post office was open between ten and noon Christmas morning.

Obediently, on December 25 Mary walked down to the post office with her older brother Enrico. Mary showed the postmaster her note. Inside the post office were dozens of toys and gifts, money tied around a doll, mitts, socks, and a hat to keep Mary warm in the winter. Thank heavens she had brought her bigger brother along to help her carry everything home!

At 92, Mary still makes her home in Trail and can recall that special Christmas with crystal clarity.

"I was six when my father died," she said, "and I remember that Christmas like it was yesterday."

The Magic of It All
Could anything be more memorable than Christmas stocking treats and presents under the tree? One of three little girls living near Peachland at the turn of the century, Adelaide Treasure discovered there was more to Christmas than gifts. There could be magic as well.

"One Christmas I went with another girl, to stay with a little girl by the name of Mary Miller," Adelaide began. "They lived way, way up in the mountains. They had a big ranch up there. They wanted to have some other little girls there for Mary's sake, because she was an only child, you see. The other girl's name was Jean Pollard. We went in a sleigh, all covered up with fur rugs in the back to keep us warm. It was a long trek up that mountain, I'm telling you, in deep snow. It's a wonder the horses ever got up there."

The Millers had a large Christmas tree all decorated by the time the little girls climbed down from the sleigh. This was the night Santa was to come. That was exciting enough, but when Mrs. Miller announced that when Santa arrived, she would come in and wake the girls so they could visit with him, all hope of sleep was banished.

Not long after the three girls were tucked into the one big bed, the silence outside was broken by the sound of bells. Mrs. Miller hurried into the bedroom. Look out the window, she urged. The girls scraped little holes in the frost-covered windows.

"I can remember peering through these little holes that we'd made, wiping them off, to see him," Adelaide recalled. "We went out and here was Santa Claus standing by the fireplace, with a great big sack of all kinds of stuff. We wanted him to stay and have breakfast with us, and he said, 'oh, [I] couldn't possibly do that', because he had to go to Peachland before a certain time, you see.

"Mrs. Miller said that if we went back and looked through the window we would see him leave. Well, they must have taken deer horns and put them on the horses, and when he was leaving the bells were ringing and he was waving to us.

"It was really a fantastic thing. They went to an awful lot of trouble. It was a fantastic Christmas. I can't remember any child ever having a Christmas like it."

Does the magic of a child's Christmas exist today? Perhaps it still does, if you are a child, if you believe. Kids don't talk about it, and won't, until 40 or 50 years later. Then, they smile and say, "I remember this one Christmas ..."

And they relive the magic all over again.

Chapter 5
Gift-Giving Magic

xchanging gifts is a major part of the Christmas season. From searching for that perfect item, to wrapping it up in festive paper and placing it under the tree, the steps of gift-giving have become holiday customs unto themselves. Of course, some of the most treasured holiday gifts are the ones that cannot be wrapped. Instead, they come in the form of kind words, bighearted gestures, or generous donations.

Gold and Christmas Giving

In 1858, a twist of fate changed the colony of Vancouver Island forever and ended its dependence on the fur trade: gold was discovered on the Fraser River. For the '49ers and those who had followed them to the California gold fields, the news of the find had 20,000 dreamers and schemers fighting their way aboard every kind of ship and boat that could carry them north to the tiny British colony. They weren't all bent on digging and sluicing. Men had to be equipped, had to be clothed, had to eat, and, when the winter chased them down through the Fraser Valley back to Victoria, they had to have places to live. So, while the adventurous tramped upriver, the enterprising — the merchants, tradesmen, and builders — set about building a city on the slopes beyond the fort's bastions.

Everybody was, quite literally, from "somewhere else," and at no other time of the year were bitter regrets mingled so poignantly with fond memories as they were at Christmastime. Publisher Amor de Cosmos, self-proclaimed Lover of the Universe, exploited these feelings effectively in his Christmas editorial in his newspaper, the *British Colonist.* "From the cradle to the grave," he wrote, "Christmas always presents pictures of family re-unions, social endearments and universal festivity. It is the season when the benevolent always remember the needy; the old wardrobe becomes warm and new; the scanty table partakes of plenty; the sick and distressed are comforted ..."

The "benevolent" of de Cosmos's editorial were none other than the new citizens of the burgeoning city, and their spirit of giving would glow most brightly in December of 1861. Miners had now followed gold's lure hundreds of kilometres up the exhausting Harrison-Lillooett trail into the wilds of the Cariboo. That meant the trip back to Vancouver Island to escape winter's freezing clutches was now longer and more arduous than ever. Upon their arrival in Victoria, many who had journeyed from Antler Creek, Williams Creek, and the tent settlement that would be Barkerville, were already ill. Others would soon become so. A Christmas fundraiser was organized to help those lying in hospital beds. Under the authorship of "Santa Claus," the city's newspaper published a Christmas Day poem to help encourage the generosity of its readers.

> Here is to your Christmas joys,
> Ye gallant ones and true,
> Ye merry boys, ye jolly boys,
> The boys of Cariboo.
> And here's to wives' elation,
> So they be leal and true,
> And here's to those awaiting
> The boys of Cariboo.
>
> Were I a woman young and smart,
> And lovely as I'm true,
> I know I'd keep a faithful heart
> For one from Cariboo.
> Here's to the nuggets you have got,
> And those that yet remain,
> They ne'er shall bless the lout or sot,
> But be the brave man's gain.

Gift-Giving Magic

The manly sons of manly toil,
The stalwart and the true,
Whether they plough the main or soil,
The boys of Cariboo.
And as to those who have no gains,
I would my song were gold,
And I would buy up all their gain
As quickly as 'twas told.

But, ah! For those, the sick and weak,
That in a darkened room
Have no kind wife to fondly speak,
And kiss away their gloom,
I would I were a prophet now,
To whisper in each ear,
Calming each fever heated brow—
"Look up, the boys are near.

"There is not one e'er sunk a shaft,
But kindly thinks of you,
Remembering how in hope's fair craft,
Ye cruised for Cariboo.
With helping hand and cheering voice
They've come to succor you."
The kindly boys, the friendly boys,
The boys from Cariboo.

Christmas Shopping — Victorian Style

Though it can be hectic and frustrating, shopping for Christmas gifts and other holiday items has long been an important part of the season. In Victoria's early days, storekeepers did what they could to make the shopping experience festive and pleasurable.

"Did you know," commented Mrs. Nellie Gillespie, "the butcher shops were absolutely beautiful. They had the carcasses hanging and they had a beautiful design — they drew this design on it in some way — it was most beautifully done. All these carcasses would be hanging up in the butcher shop, and then all the turkeys and the geese and of course, wild game, too. There's nothing like that now. You never see it."

The reason was, perhaps, that in an era before refrigeration, meat was hung simply to age. "We never thought of having ice," Mrs. Gillespie said later, "so it was just hung properly in a cool place."

Beef from Goodacre's butcher shop "would come up [to their home] before Christmas all nicely cut up in about 10 or 12 15-pound joints. Those would all be given away as Christmas presents: one to the clergyman, one to the doctor and so on."

Perhaps the fact that her father, J. H. Todd, was a prominent cannery operator and grocer himself lent Nellie Gillespie's recollections a somewhat romantic hue. The "carcasses hanging" didn't impress one young girl who lived in nearby James Bay.

Gift-Giving Magic

Young Emily Carr was plainly disgusted by the headless, "dead and naked" flesh in Goodacre's window. She much preferred other sights. In her reminiscences, the artist recalled how she and her sisters would traipse across the James Bay Bridge (the site of today's Empress Hotel causeway) with her father, Richard Carr, and visit the brightly lit shops up on Government Street.

"Every lamp post had a fir tree tied to it — not corpsy old trees but fresh cut firs. Victoria streets were dark; this made the shops look all the brighter. Windows were decorated with mock snow made of cotton wool and diamond dust. Dry goods shops did not have much that was Christmassy to display except red flannel and rabbit fur baby coats and muffs and tippets. Chemists had immense globes of red, green and blue medicine hanging from brass chains in their shop windows. Castor oil in hideous blue bottles peered from behind nice Christmas things and threw out hints about over-eating and stomachache.

"In Mr. Saunders' the grocer's window was a real Santa Claus grinding coffee. The wheel was bigger than he was. He had a long beard and moved his hands and his head."

All around the Santa lay a sweet feast for childish eyes: bonbons, cluster raisins, nuts and candied fruit, and long walking sticks made of peppermint candy. Pure magic.

There was more magic inside Government Street's three toy stores. In 1888, a *Colonist* reporter said there was much for children to dream about: "the dolls, the wooly horses and the thousand and one new and novel toys. Children might wonder if it is not here that Santa Claus makes his home." For "children of larger growth" there were tool chests for boys and tea sets and china and silverware for girls.

Spiritual Gifts

For most people living a century ago, many of the rituals of Christmas were religious in nature. "Oh, yes, sure, I had to go to church," Duke Ackerman admitted. "I was all dressed up. That's the only time we had a special suit!"

This was the time of year that Sunday Schools presented their major concerts. "There'd be wonderful little plays put on and of course, Santa Claus and a huge old Christmas tree," Doris Smith recalled from her Revelstoke childhood. "Sometimes the Sunday School concert was held in the local theatre." That meant special costumes and lots of practice beforehand, she recalled. "We'd have to be all dressed up in costumes. You know, the kiddies today don't have the thrill of all that."

Victoria resident Louise Iverson remembered what she called the "Sunday School do's". These particular "do's" were held in the James Bay Methodist Church. In addition to the Christmas tree and Santa Claus, these special events meant something much more to Louise, something so meaningful, so emotional, that once it touched her life, it enriched her experience from that moment on.

"One thing I remember about Christmas, always, the

Metropolitan Church had a production of the Christmas part of the 'Messiah' at an evening service when the place was packed. When I was quite a tiny child, my mother would take me to that, and I became just engrossed in music from the time I could think. And she taught me to sing."

Louise's mother was a soloist in the church choir, but the performing — and the music —didn't end there. At home, Louise's mother would play the organ or the family's beautiful mission oak piano. Thus, the strong link between church and music was forged in little Louise, a link that would remain unbroken throughout Louise's entire life.

Louise's mother was a far better singer than she was a musician, but, her daughter recalled, "she could do enough to play the Christmas songs on the organ and then, of course, her ambition was for me to be able to do that." Her mother's ambition gradually became her own and, years later, Louise Iverson brought Christmas melodies to her own students over the years through her school choirs in Keefer, in the Fraser Canyon, Princeton, and Victoria. In later years, Louise had a companion when she went to choir practice: her nine-year-old son.

"What's all this story about angels and all the rest of these things?" he asked Louise one Christmas.

"I don't know," she said. She couldn't prove or disprove the "angels and all the rest of these things," but she did know one thing: the Christmas story had inspired some of the greatest music and art. She told her son about Bach's

Christmas Oratorio and Handel's *Messiah*. "There two things alone," she said, "are worthy of the Christmas story."

Decades later, in her seventies, Louise Iverson was still singing in Victoria's Metropolitan Church Choir and performing Handel's *Messiah*, which, so many years before, had become a turning point for a young Victoria girl.

In early December 1933, Emily Carr was nearing her 62nd birthday. "A heaviness descended upon me this afternoon, a great, black foreboding cloud," she confessed to her diary. "Why? I cannot shake it. Are those I love worried or in trouble? I cried far into the night. Why? How should I know? Just a great wanting, a longing to know and understand which way."

The anguished artist railed against what she perceived as her maddeningly elusive ability to capture, in oils, on canvas — or even with words on paper — that "intensity of experience and feeling, the existence of the thing spiritually."

"Oh, to realize that intensity!" she agonized, in the diaries that were to become the basis for the book, *Hundreds And Thousands: The Journals of an Artist.* "It is of the soul. Oh, God, give it to me! It is mine already deep within, but asleep. How can I wake it? Oh, how?".

With Christmas Day less than two weeks away, Emily attended a "New Thought" lecture. If the visiting theologian intended to lift the spirits of his audience, he failed — at least with Emily Carr.

"Dr. Ryley from the states expounded on the spiritual

mystery of Christmas or birth of Christ in the soul," Emily recounted in her diary. "Oh, goodness gracious! What is one to *believe*? Everyone thinks he is right and runs down the other fellow's religion and extols his own. God, God, God. That's what we all want, to get a nearer and better understanding of God."

Almost exactly five years earlier, Emily had been introduced to a new way to find God: through art. In a life-changing period that radically altered her outlook and increased her self-confidence, she had met members of the Group of Seven. Her relationship with Lawren Harris, her mentor in many ways, was pivotal. Their letters dealt not only with artistic matters — technique, themes, and presentation — but also with the spiritual basis for art itself. Harris was a devotee of theosophy, a structure of beliefs favoured by artists of the time. Emily threw herself into the rigors of the demanding philosophy, and attempted to be one with "the infinite."

The New Thought lecture troubled Emily. However, the very next day, it seems the experience provided the impetus for her to make a sudden and important decision. "Today, I wrote Lawren and told him I couldn't swallow some of the theosophy ideas."

Emily's decision to set theosophy aside and to tell Harris she had done so must have been a difficult one for her. She first had to separate her affection for the man and her respect and admiration for his artistic ability, from her change of heart about his spiritual beliefs. She had tried hard to understand and accept the theosophical philosophy herself, and in the end, could not. The reason harkened back to her earlier faith.

"I had to be honest," she admitted in her diary, and one can almost feel the heavy weight of indecision lift from her shoulders. "It's their attitude toward the Bible I can't endorse. It's awful to have your holy of holiest dusted with a floor rag and a stable broom."

Nor, as time went on, could she easily accept the popular concept of Christmas itself. "Silliness and sentimentality instead of holiness," she sniffed.

"Oh, Holy Babe in your manger," she wrote, as the holiday season approached the next year, "how we have spoiled your birthday and made it a greedy, toilsome time. We know it, but everybody else does the same, so we go on doing it."

In one particularly evocative passage, she wrote of her experiences on Christmas Eve, 1934. "It was still night when I set out for the cathedral's early celebration and it was raining hard and everywhere was dark and wet and mysterious. Only one or two kitchen lights and all the streetlights. Even the children had not opened the one eye that could shut out Santa and the rest of the tiredness of Christmas Eve shopping. The puddles gleamed under the street lamps and the shadow of my umbrella accompanied me all the way. There is something very holy about communion before it is light, something dark and warm and mystic in the dim corners of the Cathedral, the pine smell of the decorations, the scarlet of the poinsettia blooms. When we came out, dawn was coming, grey and wet. The street lamps were out so the umbrellas had to march alone without a companionable jogging shadow."

And at the end of Christmas Day the next year, she recounted her visit with her two remaining sisters. At last, she seemed to find a measure of peace and contentment with siblings that, for most of her adult life, had never acknowledged or encouraged her artistic ability. It was different now, and Christmas allowed them a closeness they had often denied themselves in earlier times:

We just had our present-giving at Alice's, just we three old girls [Emily, Alice, and Lizzie]. Alice's house was full of the smell of new bread. The loaves were piled on the kitchen table; the dining room table was piled with parcels, things changing hands. This is our system and works well; we agree on a stated amount — it is small because our big giving is birthdays. Each of us buys something for ourselves to our own liking, goods amounting to the stated sums. We bring them along and Christmas Eve, with kissings and thankings, accept them from each other — homey, practical little wants, torch batteries, hearth brooms, coffee strainers, iron handles, etc. It's lots of fun. We lit four red candles in the window and drank ginger ale and ate Christmas cake and new bread and joked and discussed today and tomorrow and yesterday and compared tirednesses and rheumatics and rejoiced that Christmas came only once per year. We love each other, we three; with all our differences, we are very close.

It was Lizzie's last Christmas.

Gifts From the Heart and the Hands

In the 19th century, in an era of knitting circles, quilting bees, and painstaking craftsmanship in wood and metal, people would substitute time and talent for the money they didn't have, and create gifts themselves. Often beginning months before the gift-giving season arrived, fathers would carve presents from wood. Mothers would craft a handkerchief or scarf.

If there was a doll under the tree, chances were that it, too, was handmade or, during the poverty-stricken Christmases of the Depression, "reincarnated." A little girl's old doll, was simply repainted, repaired, and re-dressed in miniature outfits that Mother would sew after the children were in bed.

In Victoria, Duke Ackerman's father, a Victorian-era sealer, drew upon what he knew best and expressed it through his unique woodworking skills. "Father used to make these model sailboats. Oh, he was good at it," Duke said proudly. "He went to sea all his life in sealing ships." The sealing schooner that Duke's father created for Christmas one year had working sails. "They were quite a size. You could sail them. They were all carved, the keel, the cabins, everything, just like the ships he was on."

Two generations later, the writer's own father, a former

chief petty officer, was doing the same thing, with the help of new power tools. Christmas morning, there it was, painted a gun-metal grey, complete with funnel and the open bridge above the moveable replica of the four-inch gun on the deck: a miniature World War II Royal Canadian Navy corvette.

Giving in Needful Times

With hard work and frugality, countless returning World War I veterans and their families bettered themselves throughout the 1920s.

"It has been a good year," the *Victoria Times* reported cautiously on the last day of the last year in the tumultuous decade. "In spite of a greatly reduced wheat crop in the west and the spectacular fall of stocks in the last week of October, Canada faces the coming year with optimism and confidence ..."

Yet, just one year later, Lieutenant Governor R. Randolph Bruce's Christmas message was a far-from-jolly reminder that things were not what they once were: "In our province blest with a generous people, we can rest assured that every care will be taken of both our unemployed and our needy ... Let us this Christmas test the truth of the saying that true happiness is only found in giving happiness to others. Let us count our blessings, rather than dwell on our adversities."

However, as the 1930s progressed and the Great Depression deepened, many families had fewer and fewer blessings to count.

Married at the tender age of 16 to a dashing, older, Vancouver fireman, but divorced just a few years later, Adelaide Treasure was, in the late 1920s, a member of a very small minority of women who would be called, two generations later, "single moms." As a mother of three — Dick, Phil, and little Norma — there was no "career path" open for Adelaide. If she wanted work, she would have to create it herself. "Norma wasn't going to school, you see, and I didn't know how I was going to look after them and work, too. I had never worked," she explained.

The house the four moved to was a large, twelve-room, two-storey home on Bidwell Street in Vancouver's West End. There was plenty of room — but not much else. Adelaide had just enough money to pay the rent. She decided to take in borders, and "do whatever I could do," to enable her to stay home and look after the children.

If you listen to the audio tapes in the BC Provincial Archives, you can hear the tone of pride in Adelaide Treasure's voice as she related her own successful efforts at self-sufficiency, half a century earlier. It took courage, ingenuity, and perhaps a little desperation.

"Do you know that we never went on relief; never once did I ever ask for relief. We just took people as they came. If they came and they wanted board and room, we gave it to them. If they just wanted a room, we just rented it to them. If somebody wanted the downstairs, we'd let them have it and we'd move upstairs. Oh, accommodating? I'll say — as long as they had a buck!"

Christmas shopping was just one more challenge that Adelaide began to meet as soon as summer was over. "Well, I used to always have a system about clothing the children. I used to get everything when they started school in September. I'd get everything they needed in winter clothing at the Hudson's Bay; I took out an account there. Then I'd try by Christmas to have that account cleared off. Then I'd get them some new things — I always got them some things that they needed, as well as some other things and toys — and then I'd clear that off. They never went without."

Adelaide went on to recall that the family always had a "little Christmas tree." And one Christmas, a particularly special present was placed beneath it. Her oldest boy, Dick, bought a little black-and-white terrier puppy as a family gift. "How he kept it a secret, I can't remember, but I think he must have left it with the neighbours or something. But anyway, when the kids went to look under the tree for their things, this little pup just popped up out of the box. And the children! I can remember they looked so ... they didn't know what to think about it!"

That Christmas — and most of the others for Adelaide's kids — was experienced without a father at home. "Well, I think the children missed their father," Adelaide admitted, "but we never made it a sad thing in our house. We just went along the best way we could, but we never were sad; we never had a sad household because of it. For one thing, I had to work too hard. I was working dreadfully hard."

Clare McAllister's family also had it hard in the 1930s. "I have many memories of the Depression," Clare recounted. "One of the things was the horror — and I mean horror — of getting a load of wood." By the 1930s, Clare was a married woman and mother of three, living in Victoria. The unemployed men followed the wood trucks, and they would knock on the door with bright hope in their faces.

"Lady, could I put your wood in?" they would ask. "I'd do it for 50 cents."

"I'm sorry, but we have to do it ourselves," Clare would answer.

Thinking back, Clare recalled, "Your heart would melt, but you couldn't give them all even a sandwich; you didn't have that much homemade bread and certainly not much to put in it."

Decades later, Clare confessed to a particular Christmas gift-giving quirk. "I tend to put toothbrushes in my grandchildren's stocking fodder." The habit went all the way back to those dark, desperate days of the Depression. "I swear, for about nine months every day, I was swallowing bristles out of a decayed toothbrush and very likely to choke on one of them and I would say, every week, 'Next week, no matter what, I'm going to get a new toothbrush.' It would cost 10 or 15 cents, but one couldn't."

Christmas was Christmas, though. And Clare felt she could make Christmas "with my two bare hands." Thousands of other parents demonstrated the dogged determination of Clare, Adelaide, and others who substituted ingenuity and skill for the money they didn't have during the Depression.

Then, as now, service clubs and the media worked diligently to help the needy at Christmastime — and to persuade others to do the same. In Victoria, the Gyro Club distributed hampers to the destitute. Archie Wills, campaign chairman, enlisted cycle-racing champion Torchy Peden to promote the Christmas cause on the city's radio station. Not all listeners were sympathetic. "We got so annoyed ... a fellow wrote a letter complaining about having no turkeys for these poor people," Archie Wills recalled. "Well, we used to get the best joints of meat and figured it far better than having turkeys." Joining the others, Archie helped make deliveries. It was a humbling and occasionally frustrating experience. Hefting 50-pound hampers up flights of stairs wasn't easy work.

"Another thing that used to annoy some of us, was, you'd go to a door, knock at the door, and there'd be a guy sitting in his kitchen, probably, with his feet up on the stove, and you'd say, 'get him out here.' He wouldn't come!" Archie remembered, with incredulity. "We'd have to carry that stuff upstairs, or into the kitchen. You did get a bit disappointed at the attitude of some men who wouldn't even help you pack them."

Things were tough for many in the city and for many more in the country. Still, people discovered that although they didn't have much, they did have each other.

"You know the Depression, in some ways, it brought people together," Notch Hill resident Henry Copeland explained. "Nobody had any money. You couldn't go anywhere. So, the local things got going again, people got visiting amongst themselves a lot more. They'd put on a dance; everybody'd go."

Turkey and all the trimmings? Perhaps ... but probably not.

"Well, they had chickens," said Henry. "Sometimes they'd get a deer, although they weren't supposed to shoot them out of season, but, during the Depression," he laughed, "the game warden was smart: he stayed in town! No, there were not turkeys around there, not then. Oh, if you lived in town and had a job, you could get a turkey." Henry Copeland shook his head. "Unless you lived through the depression, you've no idea what it was like."

For years, Henry had worked, schemed, scrimped, and saved, and he finally managed to open a store at Notch Hill. "We went on good until the Depression came," he remembered. We used to stock up on lumberjack's clothes, heavy pants and jackets, crosscut saws, peeves, axes, everything." Whether by accident or design, Copeland's General Store was strategically located. "About three or four hundred lumberjacks used to come into Notch Hill and go across the lake and log for the Adams River Lumber Company."

But the loggers stopped coming when the mill shut down. Then the banks closed their doors. The door of

Copeland's General Store was still open, but fewer people were walking in. Unsold stock weighed heavily on the shelves — and on Henry's mind. When most of your neighbours were hard-up, retailing was hardly a road to riches. The Copelands owed one particular Christmas dinner to a man with debt. He paid Henry off with leghorns, and the family sat down to roast rooster. But the gifts that Christmas, and most others, were minimal.

"Buy presents?" Henry scoffed. "You made something up yourself, if you could. You couldn't afford to buy presents. Oh, I'll tell you, it was tough."

The Magical Ten Dollars
Henry Copeland's family had a battery-operated radio. It was, in the days before television or even telephones in most homes, a wonderful link to the outside world. That is, as long as there were batteries to light up the tubes and reach out to bring the world in through the speaker. This was a generation before the small, lightweight radios of the 1950s and 1960s. The first battery-operated radios were big — and expensive. One year, the Copeland radio fell silent. And somehow, that cold, silent radio became the embodiment of all the family's frustrations and perceived failures.

However, Henry had promised his children that the family would have music for Christmas. One day he went into town to visit a friend who operated a service station. The station had batteries for sale. Henry arranged to buy the

$10-batteries on credit until New Year's Eve.

"As long as you pay me by New Year's, you can have a couple," the operator said nervously, "but be sure to pay me by New Year's or I'm in Dutch!"

"I'll pay you somehow, I don't know how, but I'll pay you," Henry remembered telling him. Now, added to all his other worries, he had another weight to bear: the $10 he owned his friend at the service station. Soon, there was something more: his wife's outrage.

Mrs. Copeland had been hoping that a little extra business at the store around Christmastime would provide her with money for Christmas presents for the children. There was no room on her gift list for radio batteries, and now there was $10 less for the items that were already on the list. This meant she would not be able to buy most of them. At a time when men were being paid eight dollars for a month of relief work, a $10 bill represented a considerable sum.

With Christmas around the corner, Henry was sweeping up the store at the end of another day when something caught his eye, something that, as he recalled, "looked like a dollar bill." Thinking it was impossible that someone would lose a dollar during these desperate times, he swept the dust from the other direction, and there, among the pile of dirt on the floor, was the bill. Henry picked it up and was instantly thunderstruck. What he was holding in his hand was a $10 bill.

"Well, I knew nobody local had a $10 bill to lose, so it

must have come in 'off the road.' Somebody had dropped it in the store."

Here was the money to pay for the batteries, Henry thought. Then he had another thought. His wife had already "cooled down" from her anger over his decision to buy the batteries, but this lucky find was just the thing to smooth over the whole affair once and for all. He locked up the store and hurried home.

Mrs. Copeland was wide-eyed with amazement. Henry hid the money away and needlessly urged her to tell no one. "You daren't say anything," he told her, "because everybody would have lost the $10 bill!"

The next few days were long ones, indeed. Henry was on tenterhooks, waiting for some desperate friend or neighbour to dash into the store and start looking around the floor, to plead for help in finding the lost treasure. But nobody reported any missing money. Henry's assumption appeared correct. In his mind, that settled it. It was finder's keepers. The money was his, "... and we had music for Christmas."

Just before New Year's, Henry made a surprise visit to his friend at the service station and made good on his promise to pay him for the batteries that gave his family that special gift of Christmas music.

Chapter 6
Unforgettable Christmases

hough each is special in its own way, some Christmases are inevitably more memorable than others. Over the years, people throughout British Columbia have experienced Christmases filled with calamity and heartbreak, joy and excitement, action and adventure. Though they may have been heart-rending or distressing at the time, these Christmases often turn out to be the ones we remember; the ones that we talk about — and maybe even laugh about — years later.

A Christmas Miracle

At the time the Puget's Sound Agricultural Company was establishing Craigflower, Hillside, and other farms, Victoria's Inner Harbour actually extended much farther inland than it does today. Long before the causeway in front of the Fairmont Empress existed, there was a bridge that straddled the waters of the harbour, joining what is now Belville Street with the junction of Wharf Street and Government Street. In the 1850s, though, not even the bridge had been built. At the present site of the Royal BC Museum and legislative buildings, dark stands of fir and cedar stood, shrouded in the smoke from Native village fires. One Christmas Day, a mother tended one of those fires while her baby slept peacefully in her cradle-board nearby.

Suddenly, a giant bird swooped down, its talons extended, and the mother watched in horror as it snatched up the child. She screamed and her family raced to her side, only to see the gigantic bird wing its way across the harbour, in the direction of Fort Victoria. The men gave chase, but lost valuable time because there was no quick way across the harbour's water — they were forced to detour around the bay. HBC workers at the fort joined in the frantic search. Today, such a search would be easy: simply run up Yates or Fort Street. But where those streets are today, narrow muddy trails meandered through tangled rainforest.

Hope faded with the daylight. By nightfall, the rescuers were lighting torches, but soon, the search was called off; it was obvious that nothing could be seen. The next morning at daybreak, the search continued. Then, as the group was about to give up, they spotted the baby, miraculously unharmed, still strapped inside the cradle. The HBC called the site Lake Hill. Now, 150 years later, that area of the city of Victoria is known as Christmas Hill, in remembrance of that long-ago Yuletide miracle.

Icy Terror

Wartime patriotic fervour called many pioneers away from their ranches, farms, and the lonely solitude of the northern wilderness to travel to "Blighty" and then to France to fight "The Boche." When war broke out, Cliff Harrison and his brother, Bill, were trappers operating south and west of what is now Burns Lake. Cliff left to join up. Miraculously, in 1919, he returned to his brother and the Lakes Country. Cliff Harrison had survived all the horrors of the "war to end all wars," but he was fated to have his closest brush with death his very first Christmas back in the pristine wilderness of British Columbia.

The two brothers looked at their piles of furs and decided they had enough to justify the trip to buyers at Burns Lake. Besides, it was Christmas Day, a day to shake off the isolation and spend some time with other people. They poled up the White Sail River to the foot of White Sail Lake. The lake — at least at that end — was frozen solid.

"We put our boat on the sleigh with all our supplies and our equipment," Cliff remembered, "and then we proceeded on up the lake, and the ice didn't appear to be too sound or too safe, so I kept testing it. I'd go ahead possibly 50 or 60 yards and I'd take the axe to get the thickness of the ice. We were doing quite well. We got up about a mile, possibly a mile and a half and the ice appeared to me to be getting very, very clear."

Without warning, catastrophe struck.

"Everything just exploded," Cliff recalled. "Great sheets of ice broke up in front of me and in I went."

It was about 30 below zero when Cliff went through the ice and into the numbing water. As the ice fractured around him, he glanced back and saw his brother frantically scrambling toward him with the sleigh. Using his upper body as a lever, Cliff managed to roll onto a larger cake of broken ice where he lay panting for breath. The ice held him above water until Bill drew up as close as he dared with the sleigh. Cliff pushed himself to the edge of the hole, and as carefully as possible, Bill pulled him onto the sleigh.

"We've got to get to shore as quickly as we can," Cliff gasped to his brother, "because I can't live very long under these conditions, and I know that I'm going."

Bill began pushing the sleigh as hard and as fast as he could toward the shore, three-quarters of a kilometre away. Shivering inside his sodden clothing, each second seemed an eternity for Cliff. By the time the sleigh nudged the gently sloping shoreline, what little body heat Cliff had left was dissipating quickly.

"We've got to get a fire going," Bill gasped frantically.

Encased in stiffening, icy clothes, Cliff blinked and looked around. Four feet of snow hid whatever firewood might have been lying about. With the spectre of death staring into his frost-encrusted face, Cliff made a desperate decision. In front of his uncomprehending brother, he threw off the furs that covered him and began to struggle to his feet.

"I gotta keep moving!" he grunted. "Bill, if you can strap the snowshoes on me, I'm gonna try it. Before you could get a fire going, I'd be frozen to death." He swung hard and thumped his fist against his thigh. "There's no feeling in my legs! We've got to work fast."

Bill didn't argue. Shoving aside the furs in the sleigh, he extricated Cliff's snowshoes. As Cliff leaned his shuddering body against a nearby tree, Bill knelt down and began wedging his brother's feet through the straps.

The moment his brother was finished, Cliff turned and began to lurch away, ploughing through the snow between the trees. After a moment's hesitation, Bill grabbed at his own snow-shoes and quickly followed.

Breaking snowshoe trail is arduous work, even for someone in peak condition. Just a few minutes later, the half-frozen trapper was stumbling and gasping for breath. The temptation to give up, to simply relax and drift away in welcome, painless slumber was overwhelming.

A few steps behind, Bill watched his brother fearfully and shook his head. "Let me go ahead and break," he offered.

"No, no!" Cliff shouted, shrugging off his brother's hand. "I've got to do it. I've got to get this circulation coming back!"

After a quarter of an hour, Cliff could feel a telltale tingling around his knees. A few minutes later, the uncomfortable tingle had turned to searing, burning pain. Cliff winced in agony, and then began to smile through his tears. The pain was good! It meant the circulation was coming back. Yes, he thought, he just might make it.

Cliff and Bill Harrison made their way six kilometres through the snow. Their destination was the cabin of two fellow trappers, Al Price and Tom Crawford. Bill didn't wait to knock. He simply ran past his brother to the door and threw himself inside. Stunned, Al and Tom rose from the table and dashed across the room to the open door. Tom caught the stumbling form of Cliff Harrison in his arms and knew immediately what had happened.

"My heaven, you've gone through the lake!" he shouted.

"Yes," Cliff mumbled, trying desperately to hold on to a vestige of his composure. "We've had quite a bad experience down there..."

Together, Al and Tom led Cliff to the front of an old box heater. The men attempted to remove Cliff's stiff, unyielding clothing, but gave up. Cliff stood wreathed in a fog of vapour while his clothes thawed, clutching a mug of hot coffee in his shaking hands.

Al and Tom had just finished their Christmas dinner. Pots and pans rattled as Al busied himself gathering together and reheating leftovers for their two unexpected visitors. Tom, who was the same size as Cliff, brought out a suit of clean, dry Stanfield underwear and a pair of mackinaw pants. Before long, Cliff's own clothes lay steaming in a puddle of water on the rough-hewn flooring in front of the heater, and all four men were sitting around the table.

"It was," Cliff recalled half a century later, "the most memorable feed I ever had. They had killed some wild mallards early that fall, going in, and somehow or other they kept them and they had wild cranberries and they had fruit and they had potatoes, and it was just one of those feeds out of this world."

Cliff Harrison lived to see many, many more Christmases, but Christmas 1919 was one he would never forget. "I just say that the Lord wasn't ready for me yet and didn't have room for me and so I survived it."

The Chilco Curse

Gertrude Minor Roger would probably have not have called it a curse. She was far too practical, far too level-headed, to give any credence to that spooky sort of nonsense.

It started with a phone call. "Gertie" had taken the call in the ranch house near Saskatchewan's Great Sand Hills. On the other end, her husband, John Minor, could barely contain his excitement: he had found a new home for them. Angry and discouraged at the possibility of the Saskatchewan government changing the land lease policy — perhaps they would not be renewed when the current leases expired — the prosperous rancher had been scouting properties in BC.

Pulling up stakes was an enormous decision — John's father had settled the land in Saskatchewan back in the late 1800s. Now, more than 70 years later, it was time for a new start. Gertie, John, and the kids were moving to the Cariboo.

Gertie first saw the Chilco ranch from the air, in the owner's private airplane. The experience was nothing new. John had purchased his first airplane back in the late 1940s, as a proactive investment strategy in time-saving ranch management. Gertie was slow to accept flying, but she grew to appreciate the advantages of the single-engine aircraft and, with John as the pilot, became an avid passenger. That day in 1961, the Cariboo spread that Gertie looked down on — the Chilco Ranch — was the third-largest cattle spread in North America.

The Chilco, a property that actually included a number of ranches, was an immense million-acre estate with a small village of buildings. One of those buildings was a large 50-year-old store — complete with pot-bellied woodstove — which had built its business on the slogan, "Everything from a needle to a wagon." The nearby ranch house was a palatial white two-storey affair. For Gertie, as it had been for John, it was love at first sight.

In spite of her enthusiasm, Gertie thought it was strange that the ranch had been bought and sold so many times since first settled in 1886. Indeed, the property had seen a surprising number of owners. "I was beginning to wonder about all those owners," Gertie recalled later in her book,

Lady Rancher. "Maybe we would be biting off more than we could chew."

She was shocked when the present owner, a Californian by the name of John Wade, told her that, in addition to those who tried to expand too fast or didn't have the know-how to run a major spread, there was another mysterious owner who had been involved in "a bit of gunplay" and a killing in 1930. Fascinated, Gertie pressed Wade for details, and the bizarre tale unfolded.

Thirty years before, having driven out to one of the ranch's many properties with his foreman and storekeeper, the former owner impulsively leveled his shotgun and shot his foreman in the back. The crazed owner then whirled around and took aim at the storekeeper, blasting him in the arm. After that, the man simply ran off. The wounded store- keeper stayed to take the last will and testament of the dying foreman. Although weak from loss of blood, he then man- aged to lever himself into the pickup truck and attempted to drive to the main ranch. He didn't make it, but managed to flag down a ranch vehicle, driven, ironically, by the owner's wife. It was three months before the murderer's body was discovered on a Chilcotin River sandbar.

Stunned at the macabre story, Gertie couldn't help but wonder how long she and John would operate the ranch before some disaster overtook them. Her question would be answered sooner than she expected. The Minors became the Chilco's new owners on January 1, 1962.

John bought himself a new, twin-engine Comanche airplane, and Gertie brooded. Wasn't the old plane safer? The next summer, she awoke one night drenched in sweat. She had dreamed she was attending John's funeral. A week later, the nightmare returned and she awoke sobbing. Then, on November 18, wearing his Christmas present — a knitted sweater Gertie decided he should have early — John opened the front door of the house and turned back to her. He was just moments from taking off to Vancouver to pick up their two new partners. Usually there was a goodbye kiss and a joke about flying "low and slow." Not this day. Without a word, John turned around and headed out of the house toward the small hanger. Gertrude didn't watch the plane take off, and she never saw John again. His funeral was in Medicine Hat. For Gertie, it was a chilling experience of déjà-vu. "I realized I'd seen this exact scene before in my dream," she recalled. After the funeral, the widowed woman returned to the myriad of concerns, duties, and decisions awaiting her at the Chilco.

A month later, it was Christmas. In an atmosphere of renewed happiness, Gertie and the kids hosted a number of friends and acquaintances on Christmas morning. By early afternoon, the aroma of Christmas dinner was wafting through the house. Together with her son, Barry, and the son of a friend, Gertie sat in the warmth of the kitchen as Anna, their cook, prepared the year's most important dinner.

Suddenly, shouts of "Fire!" cut through the calm.

Everyone dashed to the windows. Outside, people were running frantically for hoses and buckets. Heavy black smoke belched skyward: the old store was ablaze. Within minutes, the cold, crisp air was rent with explosions as the fire's heat blew apart canned goods and exploded shotgun shells and rifle cartridges. The flames intensified as they fed hungrily on cleaning fluid and paint.

The ranch house door flew open, and firefighters urged the cowering group outside. The fire was nearing the store's gas tanks. If the tanks went up, so would the house.

Gertie and the others drove up the road where they stopped, got out, and looked down solemnly at the conflagration. Fortunately, firefighters stopped the fire before it reached the tanks. The house, at least, was spared. Disheartened and depressed, they all returned home. The power was out. Reluctantly, the dispirited family and friends sat down to a cold, dried-out, Christmas dinner by candlelight.

Six weeks later, a near-fatal head-on collision with a logging truck sent family members who were visiting from Medicine Hat racing to Williams Lake hospital. It was two weeks before one of the young passengers in the car regained consciousness. Finally, the lady rancher decided she'd had enough.

By fall, Gertie and her children were on their way back to Saskatchewan to start their life again in the familiar Great Sand Hills.

What Day Is It?

Cathy English, manager of the Revelstoke Museum and Archives, remembers her father, Charles, telling a sad story that took place on Christmas Day 1920, when he was still kid.

Life was difficult for the Harrison family, who, like thousands of other English families, journeyed to Canada just after World War I to start a new life. After a few months in Calgary, the Harrisons made a deal on a "country cottage" and an "orchard" somewhere in the Slocan Valley. The property was called Appledale, and it sounded idyllic. Of course, none of the family had ever seen it. In the late fall, father and son packed up and headed west to their new land — the rest of the family would come later.

Sadly, the country cottage turned out to be a cow shed, and the orchard, nothing more than a swamp. Nevertheless, the work began, from sun-up to long past sundown. Charles Harrison, a boy at the time, remembered being cold almost all the time. He and his father, Campbell, were not prepared for a Kootenay winter.

One day, Campbell asked his son to go to the store to buy some supplies. It was a long and difficult walk from the homestead. Then, to make matters worse, when Charles reached the store, much to his dismay, he found it was locked up tight. On his long walk back, he met a man and asked him why the store was closed.

"Why, it's Christmas Day!" the man exclaimed.

Charles was stunned. He'd had no idea. As he walked on

A poster celebrating the splendor of
Canadian food goods at Christmastime

his despondency turned to frustration, then to anger.

"Where's all the supplies?" his father asked when he saw him walk up empty-handed.

"It's Christmas Day!" the boy shot back.

"Oh, well," his father shrugged, turning back to yet another chore. "Happy Christmas, then."

"Yeah, some Christmas!" Charles shouted, and ran, crying, into the nearby woods. He stayed out there all day, in the cold, then came back to the house that night. To keep warm, he heated up some rocks to put into his bed and tried to get some sleep.

Those looking for a happy ending to this story won't be disappointed, although it came many years later. Cathy recalls that the young boy — now her father — would tell this story on Christmas Day, finishing off with, "and now, I have a warm, comfortable house, a delicious dinner on the table and my family all around me. What more could anyone want?"

"Air Mailed" Home

Phylis Bowman got the good news: her furlough had come through — over Christmas, yet! That meant there was a chance that the member of the Canadian Women's Army Corps could be home for holidays. "Home" for Phylis was Prince Rupert, and while her Christmastime furlough wouldn't have meant nearly the same thing if Phylis had been posted on the Prairies, Ontario, or the East Coast, she was stationed in Victoria. That meant, with a little luck and planning, she could spend some time with friends and family.

Of course, the odds were good that she would spend almost as much of her furlough travelling back and forth as she would in Prince Rupert. In 1943, travel was anything but fast. It was even worse during wartime holiday periods, with so many people eager to return to home and family. Train and bus stations were jammed days before Christmas. Still, Phylis was more fortunate than most, she had a choice (train or coastal steamship), and her trip was far shorter than that of many Canadian servicemen and women who endured thousands of kilometres of tedious travel in the hope of spending a day or two with loved ones.

Before leaving, Phylis shared her good fortune with an air force friend who suggested another, much faster, travel option. Why not fly up the coast with the regular weekly mail plane from Vancouver?

"Well, of course, I jumped at the chance," Phylis recalled a few years ago in her *Prince Rupert Daily News* column, "and on the appointed Sunday, made my way out to the RCAF base at Jericho Beach, all set to go."

At the time, Phylis was that rare breed of woman who had actually flown before. She and her cousin Jean had done a quick turn in an single-engine, two-seater five-dollar "thrill ride" at a summer fair, their hair and scarves billowing out behind them, "just like you see in the old movies," Phylis recounted.

But there was no repeat performance out at Jericho on that cold, damp, and foggy West Coast day — the city was socked in solid. All flights were cancelled. Her only choices left were train or boat. As Phylis weighed her options, a Sea Island dispatcher phoned over to Jericho. A plane was scheduled to leave from Sea Island soon. Phylis didn't hesitate. She called a taxi.

The speeding cab ride from the west end of Vancouver to the Richmond/Delta area cost Phylis the princely sum of $3.50, a significant amount at the time. When she arrived, Phylis found that the chilly fingers of fog had tightened their grip on Sea Island, as well. She could only do what everyone else was doing: sit and wait.

These were low-tech days, when people on the coast routinely flew without the benefit of radar, homing devices, flight plans, or radio contact with the tower, so when the pilot sauntered outside "to have one last squint at the sky," and blithely hollered, "Roll her out. It's clearing!" Phylis didn't even hesitate and scrambled into the plane with the crew of four.

On that long ago wartime day, just before Christmas, there were a few other things that Phylis flew without. Like a seat. Or a washroom. This was a Lockheed Lodestar, a large and roomy but cold and noisy aircraft built for cargo, not passengers. Phylis merely "settled down amongst the boxes of freight as we glided out of the hanger and took off into the wild blue yonder."

Hunkered down in the midst of piles of supplies and mail for far-flung settlements, Phylis marvelled at "majestic tall trees by the thousands pointing their spires proudly into the sky as we sailed inland, and millions of lakes and streams flashed golden in the setting sun."

Travelling inland was not the fastest route to the northern ocean-front community of Prince Rupert. Phylis was to experience the "milk-run" to end all "milk-runs," bound for her coastal destination by way of Kamloops, Prince George, and, finally, Terrace.

In Terrace, her aerial journey ended. That was not

surprising. The Lodestar was not a float plane, and Prince Rupert's airport was some years off in the future. Well, there was always the train, wasn't there?

The resourceful traveller made her way to the Canadian National Railway (CN) station, and found, to her dismay, that the passenger train was several hours late. She didn't complain. After all, there was a war on.

"But (oh, joy!) there was a long freight huffing and puffing there, all set to go on its winding westward trip through the bush to the coast," Phylis recalled. "So, I begged a ride home."

It was one heck of a ride: Phylis first sat in the fireman's seat in the "huge steam engine," as the fireman shovelled coal into the flaming maw of the firebox, and then, "went back into the caboose for coffee when we stopped to take on water for the locomotive."

Then there was another stop, this time at a road construction camp, to take on a second passenger, a bulldozer operator who had somehow broken his arm. When the train finally pulled into the Prince Rupert station, and Phylis spied an ambulance waiting for the injured worker, she knew exactly what to do. "I rode with him in the ambulance ... to the hospital. My dad's house was only a block from there."

It had been an incredible journey by cab, air, train, and ambulance. Phylis Bowman's experience was not unusual during those war years. In fact, CWAC Bowman's trip was much shorter than those of others who travelled days from far-away jetties in Halifax, airbase hangers in Trenton, and the drydocks of Brooklyn and Galveston, where Canadian ships underwent refit. For these men and women, it was worth the days of tedious, long-distance travel to spend a BC Christmas with those they loved. Phylis Bowman and all the others knew it was an opportunity that thousands more overseas did not enjoy. It was an opportunity many would never get to enjoy again.

Chapter 7

The Inspiration of Christmas

hristmas is a time for decorating trees, singing carols, enjoying feasts, and exchanging gifts. But more important, it's a time to cherish our loved ones and express good will towards others. It is a time for generosity and thankfulness. Over the years, countless British Columbians at home and overseas have done what they can to spread the spirit of the season — even during times of poverty and war.

The Worthless Mine

Newspaperman David W. Higgins knew well the symptoms of gold fever. The Halifax native had lived in San Francisco during the California rush and came north with the first prospectors in 1858. He ran a store and express office at

Yale, where, at the head of the Fraser River, steamboats disgorged thousands of hopeful prospectors. By 1860, he was back in Victoria and working for Amor de Cosmos at the *Colonist* newspaper.

On Christmas Eve day, working frantically on the next edition of the paper, Higgins was interrupted by a visitor to the office. It was obvious the attractive young woman was in desperate straits. She was from California and things had not gone well. The woman — Miss Forbes — had written a poem. Could the *Colonist* publish it? One look told Higgins that it wasn't worth inserting into the newspaper, but he didn't have the heart to tell her so.

The next day, Christmas Day, while walking back to his office with an acquaintance by the name of George Barclay (who, like Higgins, was living at the Hotel de France), the newspaperman saw Miss Forbes lingering at the office. She asked if he had decided to publish her poem. He had not and would not, and so he put her off again. As she walked away, Barclay confided to Higgins that he loved the woman and had actually proposed marriage to her when they lived in Grass Valley, California. Things had gone badly; their mine had proved worthless. Recently, Barclay had visited her at the cottage where she lived with her parents and brother and had kindly offered her money. The offer failed to impress either father or daughter, and she had dismissed him.

Barclay reached into his pocket, handed Higgins a $20 gold piece, and asked him to tell her it was in payment for her poem. Higgins did so, and Miss Forbes almost fainted at the sight of it. She would use it to buy Christmas dinner for her poverty-stricken family. Higgins offered to order dinner for her at the hotel and bring it to the cottage. Then he went further: he and Barclay were without family themselves, so he asked if they might join in the dinner. Miss Forbes consented, but, worried perhaps by her father's attitude, requested that Barclay arrive a little later, as if by accident.

Everything went as planned, and, as Higgins later wrote, a "real live, polite little Frenchman" from the hotel served a sumptuous meal, complete with claret and champagne. All in all, it was to be one of the most memorable Christmases in the lives of both men. Higgins and Barclay didn't get back to the hotel until midnight.

The very next day, Boxing Day, Barclay returned to the Forbes's squalid little cottage with a Christmas present none of the family expected. He had news from California: that worthless mine, it turned out, wasn't as barren as everyone had thought. The family was rich!

Soon after this discovery, Barclay proposed to Miss Forbes again. This time, the woman's answer, and her father's attitude, were different. Barclay returned to California with the Forbes family to start his life anew.

Yuletides in Uniform

"Just a few lines to wish you the Christmas greetings, if I were only with you all again, wouldn't we make things hum, you bet." The letter writer was a Victoria soldier, Cecil Nickelson. For the very first time in his young life, "Nick" was thousands of kilometres from his home on the West Coast of Canada and a certain young lady, Dorothea Thompson. "But as it is, I'll have to write my wishes. It seems so cold-blooded sticking them down on paper, but you'll know they are just as hearty."

That Christmas, over a century ago, Nickelson was part of a particularly cold-blooded business: war.

In South Africa, the young country's Dutch and German descendants, the Boers, had taken up arms against the British. The British called it a "rebellion." The Boers felt they were merely fighting for the land they had wrested from the wilderness. The Dutch East Indies Company had established the very first white settlement near the Cape of Good Hope a century earlier. By the 1820s, the Dutch had turned their backs on the coast — and the tide of English *Uitlanders*(outsiders) — and trekked north to established three new republics. All this did was delay the inevitable. Diamonds and the discovery of gold sealed the Boers' fate.

Cape Colony's British prime minister, Cecil Rhodes (who just happened to own the Kimberley diamond mines), underwrote a raid on the Transvaal city of Johannesburg. The Boer commandos fought the British off successfully, but the defeat only deepened British resolve. The British Empire's integrity was threatened, and the war was on. The announcement gave the 30-year-old Dominion of Canada an opportunity to act as an independent nation. Prime Minister Wilfred Laurier called for 1000 volunteers. Two weeks after hostilities began, Victoria's 5th CGA responded. The boys were off to the Transvaal.

It might have been a merry Christmas back in Victoria, but not in South Africa. Cecil Nickelson's letter attests to that:

> Oh, for one of your Mother's chair-pillows instead of a pair of boots or a saddle stuck under your head, and although I never let others know I feel it; they would say it was a pity I didn't bring a feather bed with me. The ground is getting harder every day, what will it be by Xmas? Fred spreads his handkerchief under him and remarks, 'that's better.' Imagination goes a long way, don't you think so?

In December 1900, the Canadians took part in the attack on the Boer stronghold of Parrdeberg. There wasn't much time for Christmas letter writing, but Nickelson nevertheless wrote when he could:

> We had another little scrap ... one man captured and one wounded ... my wound is all right again, although the bullet went through my tongue. It can't stop me talking, it would take a cannon-

ball to do that ... wishing you all a very Merry Christmas and lots of fun.

Yours very sincerely,
Nick

P.S. Eat an extra piece of pudding for me and write and tell me what it was like. It's the next best thing to eating it myself.

Christmas gives a special poignancy to forced separation at any time, especially so when that separation actually takes place during the holiday season itself. However, perhaps the season and the wartime circumstances were not as incompatible as might be thought. At least, that was the theory put forward in a Christmas Eve editorial in Victoria's *Daily Colonist* in 1899: "Many years have passed since the people of the Empire have had to divide their Christmas thoughts between Peace and Good Will and the operations of an army in the field. Yet, the marvelous work inaugurated by Him, whose natal day will be celebrated tomorrow, may be advanced as well by deeds done on the battlefield as by prayer in the cloister. 'I am not come to send peace, but a sword,' were his words. His prophetic eye saw that violence would have to be met by violence before a period of universal peace could be established."

If the reader had some difficulty reconciling the

dichotomy of the notion, well, that was to be expected. After all, the editorial went on, "The explanation of it all is too subtle for human comprehension..."

There was, however, consolation of another sort. "One lesson of Christmas is self-sacrifice," the editorial writer reasoned. "'Greater love hath no man,' He said, 'than that a man lay down his life for his friend.' Surely our brave-hearted fellow countrymen who have fallen on the South African battlefields or who may in days to come meet their fate fighting for their country, are animated by this 'greater love'."

More likely, they were "animated" by thoughts of simply surviving the ordeal themselves. Just 14 years after that 1899 editorial appeared, similar thoughts were espoused by the *Victoria Times* on Christmas Day during the opening phase of a newer, bigger war, the "war to end all wars." The headline read: "CANADA FOLLOWS":

> There is an old Oriental saying, 'Wherever the lion goes, thither will the whelps follow.' Early in August, the British lion went to Europe to aid and succor a little nation in its struggle for freedom and personal liberty.
>
> The first Canadian regiment has left Salisbury Plains for the front, and in fact may at this time actually be in the struggle. The honour has fallen to the Princess Patricia regiment, a well-trained

body of light horse, but the Highlanders from
Victoria and Vancouver will not be far behind...

Patriotic fervour was high, and if enterprising merchants could use it to turn a profit, well, so much the
better. In his newspaper ad, Victoria grocer H.O. Kirkam
chose an eye-grabbing, one-word headline, "VICTORY," and
added beneath it, "What great significance the word has
these days. Victory means success ... the enemy conquered,
beaten, humiliated."

The ad went on to inform Christmastime readers that the housewife's worst enemy was "the high cost
of living. We've fought the battle for her, we've conquered
that enemy."

Proof that Kirkham's was ready, willing, and able to
wage a price war on behalf of homemakers was the front-line
news that turkeys were just 30 cents a pound and Japanese
oranges were a mere 35 cents a box.

Comrades-In-Arms

The fervour got to Victoria newspaperman Archie Wills. An
"energetic young buck," as he later described himself, Archie
quit his job as marine editor at the *Times* and joined about
500 other "nice fellows" who were forming a battery in the
Parliament buildings.

In May 1916, Archie and the other nice fellows of the
62nd Battery, including friend Percy Gilson, marched down

through the crowds to Victoria's Inner Harbour, climbed up the gangway of the *Princess Charlotte* troopship, and sailed off to war.

In a scenario that would be repeated in the first years of World War II, the men were stationed in England for training, then more training, and still more training. "We were the best trained outfit you ever saw!" Wills laughed. For most of these men — some barely out of their teens — these were the first Christmases away from home.

As Christmas neared, mail was the tie that bound these homesick men to families and friends back home. Given wartime conditions, it was a tenuous tie at best.

"We had a lot of letters and the parcels came through pretty good, so we were pleased about that," Archie Wills recalled. "It was a question of when the mail would arrive, you know, shipping losses and all that, and I think there was some pilfering and some fellows would get them [the parcels] all bashed up, but I was very lucky. My wife sent me a two-pound box of Laura Secord chocolates ... every Saturday!" Thoughtfully, Mrs. Wills had chosen hard-centered chocolates to avoid mushing in the mail. Food, candy, and, of course, cigarettes were the most appreciated gifts from home.

"We used to smoke the darndest stuff over there," Wills remembered. "I think they swept it up off the floors of factories, so my parents used to send me a tin of Old Chum tobacco. You were thankful when the mail came. I was always receiving a great deal of stuff, but other fellows wouldn't get anything, so we'd split it up."

Aside from taking care of the horses — artillery batteries were horse-drawn — Christmas Day in England's Witley Camp was a pretty easy-going occasion. Upwards of 500 men sat down to a special Christmas dinner in the mess hall. On the printed menu, items were given their own military "flavour."

"We had all these different names for them; peas were 'shrapnel.' We started out with 'cordite,' which was celery; 'lyddite grenades,' that would be olives; 'limbergunner cheese'; well, the 'limbergunner' was the fellow that kept the gun in shape; 'number nine,' well, number nine was the 'opening medicine' they used to give you."

A Christmas Promise

The next year, Christmas was a far, far different affair for Wills, Gilson and the others in the 62nd Battery of the Canadian Field Artillery. By December 1917, they and thousands of other Canadians were weary, battle-hardened veterans "somewhere in France."

"My gun crew... we didn't have a very happy Christmas," Percy Gilson remembered. "Christmas morning, we were detailed to go up and take over a position." The position only had one gun, and so only Gilson's crew was ordered to the front. "It was bad timing," the veteran remembered sadly. There would be no Christmas dinner for Gilson, Wills, and the rest of the crew. The men were certainly ready to celebrate, and Percy remembered that Wills and others had done a little "Christmas shopping."

"I think — if I recall — Archie Wills and a few more went scavenging around and they were able to get a couple of pigs and a few bottles of wine."

"We were gonna lay one on," Wills said, smiling at the memory of it. "Old Wills had detailed a little raiding party... and we bought two pigs from some farmer. I took a wagon and two horses and a couple of men, and we scouted around the back areas. We bought some red wine and provisions ... special, so that it'd be a little different. We expected that since we were in a cushy spot that we'd be all right."

No such luck.

"I was a bit cheesed off because all the food is back there," Archie recalled. "They're going to have a party that night; Christmas dinner and it would be fairly good, and here we are, he [Percy Gilson] and I were walking down the road together."

"It was a very, very cold day," Gilson recalled, "and we had no more or less than just our little morning rations with us, which was a piece of bread and perhaps a tin of bully beef ... and we stopped on the road for a rest and I turned to Archie and I said, 'Archie, if we ever live through this, I will always phone you on Christmas Day and jack up your memory on it."

That promise, made that Christmas Day between

two mud-splattered soldiers on the road to the front line, was kept faithfully every Christmas morning for over half a century. Unfortunately, neither one of the men needed to have their memories refreshed. The day was, sadly, memorable enough.

"Some say that Christmas Day was quiet and that all guns ceased," Percy Gilson said, shaking his head. "But that is not right."

Not then. During the very first Christmas on the front, three years before, there had been an informal camaraderie between opposing forces with scarcely a shot fired on Christmas Eve. Christmas Day, mud-splattered Germans and Canadians had lifted themselves out of their trenches and stood shaking hands and exchanging season's greetings in the middle of no-man's land.

But by 1917, things had changed. As Christmas neared, Canadians were recovering from the death and destruction of Passchendaele, an objective the British failed to take and then insisted the Canadians try, although there was no strategic advantage to be gained. The Canadians succeeded, but at a cost of 16,000 casualties. That Christmas the mood was much different than it had been in 1914.

"That day we got strafed very bad," Gilson recalled as he shook his head sadly. "We took over the gun position and started in right away in retaliation." Somewhere in the world during that winter of 1917, there was a feeling of peace and good will towards men, but not in Flander's fields.

"What can you do?" Archie Wills asked, over 60 years after his Christmases at the front. "You can't get up and walk back and say, 'I'm sick of this stuff.' Your orders are there and ..." The elderly veteran paused and narrowed his eyes. "The old men like me, these are the guys that should fight the wars, if they're going to have them, because one night outside in the open and you'd be ready to call it quits by morning."

Christmases Back Home

During war years — it doesn't matter what war it was — in countless homes all over British Columbia, Christmas was a day of decidedly mixed feelings. When presents were opened on Christmas morning, there was often one or more of the family who could not share the laughter and taste the eggnog. When Christmas dinner was served, there were empty chairs around the table. Brothers, fathers, husbands, uncles, and nephews were "at the front."

A youngster at the time, Duke Ackerman felt the absence of his older brother. It made no difference that the family was a large one, and that there were four other brothers and sisters around the dinner table December 25. "You knew where he was at and that's all. You know, you couldn't do nothing about it. Christmas went on just the same, just the same as now."

Clare McAllister's brother was also absent at Christmastime during World War I. "My brother, was, to me, of course, a hero," Clare explained.

Her brother, Donald McQuarrie, joined the army before he was even 18 years old. Wounded twice, McQuarrie was awarded the Military Cross and was made captain. Donald was missed most as Christmas approached. "I can remember the fabrication of parcels that were sent very frequently to my brother. One thing we did was dip the scarlet maple-leafs in melted paraffin. This preserved the colours and a few of these were then laid on top of a parcel."

Christmas 1918 was the saddest one of all for Clare and her family. Captain McQuarrie was killed just six weeks before the armistice.

Like Clare and her family, and countless others, those back home waited. They waited for him — or sometimes her — to step off the train, to walk down the gangway, to jump from a cab, home again, at last! In the meantime, they waited for the mail. In rural areas, men and women stepped into the post office, key in hand, and held their breaths: today there might be a letter. Even when they knew he or she was a POW, they waited. Sometimes the wait was rewarded.

In cities like Victoria and Vancouver, where mailmen made their rounds (sometimes, twice a day), mothers and wives synchronized their activities so that they would be home when the envelopes slid through the mail slot and fell to the floor, or when there was a knock on the door. Perhaps it was a big parcel, received with as much relief as excitement.

"Dear Moms," RCAF flying officer Donald McCulloch began, just two weeks before his first Christmas away from the Okanagan Valley. McCulloch was writing between bomber missions with the 61st Squadron, agonizing missions that took him and so many others through a deadly curtain of flak to their targets in Germany.

> Remember those other Christmases, Mother? The Christmas cakes, the Oregon grape and holly dug from under the snow — walking miles through bushes to cut a suitable tree...

> Remember the excitement over the ceremonial decorating of our tree? The ancient dust covered boxes were brought forth from the cellar where they had rested peacefully for a year. They were opened & 4 anxious children examined their contents critically; choosing this, discarding that. The endless lengths of faded tinsel & the contrastingly glittering newly-bought-that-week. The dozens of ornaments, the miniature Santa Clauses, Adam & Eve, the strings of tree lights (which varied every year with Dad's replacements).

> ... And best of all there was Xmas day to come; Xmas day when one carried the "little tree" & presents over to Grannie's, Xmas day with its parcels to be unwrapped, explored & appraised. The carols, the millards of nuts, sweets, cakes, feasts — a wonderful

day. The most wonderful of a child's year!

Mother and Dad, I thank you for those glorious spontaneous Xmases; for what they meant to that child; and what they mean now to this slightly older edition of him.

All my love,
Donald.

A few months later, there was another knock at the door. The dreaded telegram had come to Donald's family: "Missing in action." Confirmation arrived just a couple of months before the next Christmas. Donald McCulloch would not be returning home.

A New Start
As many reminiscences make clear, Christmases were not always "merry and bright." For newcomers to Canada, for those returning home from war, and for those who were suffering economic deprivation, the emotionally charged and expectation-laden Christmas season was always an especially challenging time. However, resourceful, determined, and imaginative people rose to the challenge, over and over again.

Having survived World War I as a member of the Fifth Western Cavalry, Henry Copeland sat on the train and contemplated his future. What future? Henry had sold his farm in Paton, Saskatchewan, before he left Canada to go overseas.

"I didn't know whether I was coming back or not," he later joked.

Well, now he was back. In October 1919, he and his wife stepped off the train in Manitoba to visit his sister. The visit was a great excuse, and the couple had a place to stay for free, but the real reason for the trip was to allow Henry to assess prospects for starting over again. But timing, they say, is everything. Farms were already in the grip of winter. The memories came flooding back, and not all of them were pleasant. Henry shook his head.

"I'm not staying down here," he told the women. "I'm getting the heck out of this country. I'm going up to Vancouver."

Once in Vancouver, Henry thought his luck had turned. Just by chance, he ran into an officer he had known in France. When Henry mentioned he was a man searching for a new start and a new place, his wartime acquaintance mentioned that he knew of a farm that had just foreclosed. That was interesting news, but the former army officer also had a tip: Henry could probably buy it under the federal government's new "Returned Soldiers" program. The farm was located near Notch Hill, east of Kamloops.

"It was 20 acres cleared and there was a house on it. And the house was what I was after. Some place to live."

The deal was made and the Copelands moved in just

before Christmas. Before long, they had a visitor. A representative of the Soldiers' Settlement Board paid a call. It wasn't a benevolent gesture. The government man's mission was to assess the Copelands' financial situation. Under the scheme, the Board could claim 50 percent of the farm's profit. Henry knew why the man was there, and he simply told him that he would just stop earning any money altogether.

The representative nodded. He was a veteran, too, like Henry. He was sympathetic. "And he says, 'I haven't seen anything, I don't know anything', and that was that." The man's understanding was probably the best Christmas present the Copelands could have asked for.

"We just celebrated ourselves," he recalled. "We didn't know anybody." The present was bleak, but it was the future they concentrated on. "We were looking forward to spring, you know, and getting something going. And we did. I got some cows and chickens," Henry reminisced years later.

Over time, Henry and his wife made friends with others in the area, including World War I veterans like himself. A few years after they first settled in Notch Hill, when they got together with neighbours for Christmas, one of the dinner guests was an old Scotsman who made smooth, potent cider, and sold it for a dollar a gallon. After Christmas dinner, out came the cards — and the Scotsman's jug. As the night progressed the jug became lighter and lighter.

"Well, there's not much left, we might as well finish it," the Scotsman said. Henry remembered well what happened next.

"So, when he tilted the jug, out fell a mouse. No hair on it! All raw," Henry laughed many years later. "We'd been drinking that all the way through Christmas ... but nobody got sick." Still, Henry added, "I never drank cider out of a brown jug again."

A Christmas lesson learned and never forgotten!

Bibliography

Adams, John. "Christmas In Old Victoria." *Discover The Past*, 2003.

Berton, Pierre. *The Last Spike*. Toronto: McClelland & Stewart, 1971.

Carr, Emily. *Hundreds And Thousands,* from *The Emily Carr Omnibus.* Vancouver: Douglas & McIntyre Ltd., 1993.

Carr, Emily. *The Book Of Small.* Toronto: Irwin, 1966.

Grescoe, Audrey and Paul. *The Book Of War Letters.* Toronto: McClelland & Stewart, 2003.

Mole, Richard. *Seasons Greetings From British Columbia's Past.* Victoria: Provincial Archives of British Columbia, 1980.

Roger, Gertrude Minor. *Lady Rancher* Saanichton: Hancock House, 1979.

Acknowledgements

The author's thanks to the helpful personnel in the following archives: Provincial Archives of British Columbia, Greater Victoria Public Library; McPherson Library of the University of Victoria, Vancouver City Archives; Prince Rupert City and Regional Archives (Barbara Sheppard, Archivist); Revelstoke & District Historical Association (Cathy English, Manager/ Curator); Bulkley Valley Museum (Jane Young, Curator), Nelson Museum (Shawn F. Lamb, Director); Greater Vernon Museum and Archives (Linda Wills, Archivist); and Trail City Archives (Samantha Poling).

All oral reminiscences included in this book are part of the permanent collection of the Sound and Moving Image Division of the Provincial Archives of British Columbia: Duke Ackerman, No. 3582; Henry Copeland, No. 3577; Percy Gilson, No. 3580; Louise Iverson, No. 3579; Clare McAllister, No. 3578; Adelaide Treasure, No. 3552; and Mr. and Mrs. Leo Hammond (Cultural Community Series) No. 54.

A special debt is owed by the author — and all other researchers — to broadcaster Imbert Orchard, whose extensive collection of historical interviews contributed the remaining reminiscences: Sarah Bourgon, No. 1202; Cecilia Bullen,

Acknowledgements

No. 1289; Nellie Gillespie, No. 1311; Cliff Harrison, No. 1028; Helen Hood, No. 1290; Peter Lagace, No. 760; Harry Marriott, No. 306; Major Roger Monteith, No. 1287; Madge Musket, No. 1312; Beulah Probert, No. 756; Doris Smith, No. 461; Mary Tesky, No. 779; Bunch Trudeau, No. 1783; and Bert Williams, No. 451.

Special thanks also to Phylis Bowman, Victoria (formerly, Prince Rupert).

Excerpts from *Hundreds and Thousands*, by Emily Carr, from *The Emily Carr Omnibus* published 1993 by Douglas & McIntyre Ltd. Reprinted by permission of the publisher.

"A Flypast of Christmases" taken from *The Book of War Letters* by Audrey and Paul Grescoe. Used by permission of McClelland & Stewart Ltd., *The Canadian Publishers*.

Photo Credits

About the Author

BC-born author Rich Mole has enjoyed an eclectic communications career, as a former broadcaster, a freelance journalist, and, for 20 years, the president of a successful Vancouver Island advertising agency. A lifelong fascination with history has fuelled his desire to write about the times and people of Canada's past. Rich now makes his home in Calgary, Alberta.

AMAZING STORIES™

CHRISTMAS IN ·: THE PRAIRIES ·:

Heartwarming Legends, Tales, and Traditions

HOLIDAY
by Rich Mole

ISBN 1-55153-782-6

OTHER AMAZING STORIES

These titles are available wherever you buy books. If you have trouble finding the book you want, call the Altitude order desk at 1-800-957-6888, e-mail your request to: orderdesk@altitudepublishing.com or visit our Web site at www.amazingstories.ca

New AMAZING STORIES titles are published every month.